LOCAL ECONOMIC DEVELOPMENT

LOCAL ECONOMIC DEVELOPMENT

A Guide to Practice

Emil E. Malizia

PRAEGER SPECIAL STUDIES • PRAEGER SCIENTIFIC

New York • Philadelphia • Eastbourne, UK
Toronto • Hong Kong • Tokyo • Sydney

Library of Congress Cataloging in Publication data

Malizia, Emil E.
Local economic development.

Bibliography: p.
Includes index.
1. Industrial promotion – United States. 2. Economic
development projects – United States.   3. Economic
development projects – United States-Finance.   I. Title.
HC110.I53M35   1985   338.973   84-26490
ISBN 0-03-001292-9 (alk. paper)

Published in 1985 by Praeger Publishers
CBS Educational and Professional Publishing
a Division of CBS Inc.
521 Fifth Avenue, New York, NY 10175 USA
© 1985 by Praeger Publishers

56789 052 987654321

Printed in the United States of America
on acid-free paper

PREFACE

In all U.S. localities, people express deep concern about employment opportunities, job security, and retirement incomes. Businesspeople in growing and declining industries acknowledge the greater uncertainty and volatility of the economic environment. Elected officials worry about the tax base and the costs of public goods and services. At the same time, traditional strategies of local economic development grow less workable. Industrial recruitment and promotional efforts are less successful as more money is spent and as more jurisdictions join the fray. Federal funds for local development are less available. The private sector is called upon to take the initiative. Local leaders from all sections of the country and from all positions on the political spectrum are paying attention to local economic development.

Before 1960, the concern for economic development was largely confined to the developing nations of the Third World. JFK's campaign for the presidential nomination raised our awareness of regional poverty in the United States. The Great Society programs that followed were designed to eliminate "pockets of poverty" in central city ghettos, declining rural areas, and depressed regions. The Economic Development Administration (EDA) was established to attack area poverty and unemployment. Through planning and technical assistance, grants to localities, and loan programs, EDA tried to promote local economic development on a "worst-first" basis. The Farmers Home Administration was given a similar mandate to promote development in rural areas.

Throughout the 1970s economic development became increasingly important. A variety of attempts were made to forge linkages among economic community development, small business development, and economic development programs to increase their local effectiveness amid ever more pressing budgetary constraints. States and localities were taking concrete steps to face the related problems of economic adjustment and fiscal stress. Every state had developed industrial recruitment and promotional programs to bid for the investments of U.S.-based and foreign corporations. Many localities, especially the large cities and jurisdictions in mature industrial areas, had been encouraging job creation

v

and economic revitalization for some time. Business and neighborhood organizations supported measures to increase local economic growth and development. All jurisdictions appeared to be concerned with local economic development whether their economic bases were growing, declining, stagnant, or experiencing readjustment problems.

Since 1980, the concern for local economic development has remained pervasive, but the approach has changed dramatically. At the federal level, the threat is no longer domestic social unrest but the competitive pressures of the international economy. The goals have shifted from the elimination of regional inequality and poverty to the enhancement of productivity, economic growth, and global market shares. At the state level, traditional industrial development approaches are viewed as insufficient, and new policies and programs to promote innovation and entrepreneurship and to support existing industries are being proposed. At the local level, new awareness exists that competition for federal grants and corporate facilities represents a high-risk approach to economic development. As corporate investment patterns become less predictable and domestic assistance declines, local actors from the public, private, and nonprofit sectors are assuming the lead roles in providing employment opportunities and shoring up the tax base. In a growing number of places, local leaders are looking inward for the talent, resources, and ideas needed to spur local economic development.

Elected officials in most larger cities have already accepted economic development as an important function of local government and are now rethinking public roles and responsibilities. Members of local development commissions are searching for innovative approaches to local economic development. Some localities have a municipal agency responsible for economic development. Others vest responsibility in nonprofit development organizations. Whether separate organizational entities, or part of local Chambers of Commerce or neighborhood associations, these organizations often lead local efforts. Their challenge is to promote local economic development in the face of dwindling resources and complex economic problems.

Although generalizations about new approaches to local economic development are difficult, the local roles and responsibilities are certainly creating more complex relationships. New arrangements and efforts are being described as "public–private partnerships" and "co-development." On the one hand, public–private cooperation to promote local development is not a new phenomenon. At least since the urban renewal program of the 1950s, local governments have assembled land, constructed infrastructure, and invested in public services and facilities to increase the potential and profitability of private development efforts. With grants-in-aid and tax-exempt financing, they have provided industrial parks, skills training, and loans to encourage corporate investment.

On the other hand, important aspects of the relationships are noteworthy. The local private sector, more aware of the advantages of partnership arrangements, is growing more flexible and willing to negotiate about the burdens and benefits of development projects. The nonprofit sector is de-emphasizing grantsmanship and public program administration. Its current interest is in gaining access to the resources and expertise needed to form profit-making businesses and to develop real estate projects. The local public sector is formulating economic development plans and policies in response to local, not federal, initiatives. In many cases, the returns from public outlays extended for future tax revenues are no longer considered to be sufficient. Less willing to socialize the costs and privatize the benefits of development, the public sector is seeking financial participation in development projects. This more active role is often achieved through a local development organization (LDO). In different regions of the country, LDOs are identifying potential ventures, analyzing the political, economic, and financial feasibility of alternative projects, and providing financial assistance to particular projects to meet local economic development objectives.

As a consequence of co-development and public–private partnerships that have restructured local relationships, local actors are creating new economic development opportunities. They demand a fuller understanding of the development process and sharper skills to increase the success of partnerships and co-development efforts. Fortunately, conferences, workshops, training courses, and published materials are available to assist local actors. Particularly noteworthy are the efforts of the National Council for Urban Economic Development (CUED), the Urban Land Institute (ULI), the National Association of State Development Organizations and other affiliates of the National Governors Association, the American Planning Association and the American Institute of Certified Planners, the International City Managers Association, the National League of Cities, the Corporation for Enterprise Development, and the National Federation of Independent Business. Many universities and private groups sponsor courses for local practitioners to develop specific skills. Basic economic development courses directed at industrial development professionals are being broadened in response to new local realities. However, no concise treatment of local economic development gives local actors both theoretical understanding of the economic development process and the practical skills needed to design public–private partnerships and execute local development projects. This book was written to respond to these needs.

I am indebted to many individuals who have shaped my ideas about local economic development over the past 20 years: the Chamber of Commerce staff in New Brunswick, New Jersey; faculty and fellow graduate students at Cornell University; federal policy makers, advocates, and analysts in Washington, D.C.; associates in Colombia, S.A.; and especially colleagues and students at the Department of City and Regional Planning of the University of North Carolina at Chapel Hill.

Over the past four years, I have learned much from business development clients and associates in North Carolina. The arguments presented in this book benefited from the comments of participants enrolled in three in-service training courses that were sponsored by the North Carolina Chapter of the American Planning Association. I acknowledge permission to reprint materials in Appendix B granted by the National Council for Urban Economic Development.

I thank Sarah Rubin of MDC Inc. for reviewing the book in its entirety; Rick Carlisle, Director of the North Carolina Division of Community Assistance, for supporting the original work that led to Chapters 5 and 6; Charles Roupas, president of the Village Bank in Chapel Hill, and the graduate students in my market analysis course who provided input for Chapter 8; and David Sawicki, director of the graduate city planning program at Georgia Tech, who arranged a series of lectures in Atlanta that provided a forum for discussing the ideas in this book.

I extend special thanks to David Godschalk and Michael Stegman, my past and current departmental chairpersons, for their encouragement. I am grateful for the loving support provided by my wife, Deborah Anne; and I am most fortunate to be father of the world's best daughter, Beth Sullivan Malizia.

CONTENTS

CHAPTER

LIST OF TABLES AND FIGURES

TABLE

FIGURE

INTRODUCTION

The aim of this book is to present a broad treatment of local economic development for the actors forging public–private partnerships. Local actors are the primary audience of the book. They may be placed in four major categories: (1) locally elected officials who have the responsibility for creating and funding the organizations and administrative agreements to promote local economic development; (2) professionals directly involved in local public–private development projects including private developers, business executives, bankers, attorneys, accountants, planners, architects, community and industrial developers, and public-sector managers; (3) members of local development bodies who represent business, financial, labor, or community-based organizations; and (4) consultants who offer training and technical assistance to these individuals. The secondary audiences of the book include the practitioners, graduate students, and advanced undergraduate students who want to learn the basic principles of local economic development and acquire some basic skills to become participants in local development efforts; the instructors seeking teaching materials for undergraduate-level, graduate-level, or in-service training courses; state and federal government administrators responsible for employment, community, economic, or small business development programs; and the executives and staff of the professional associations and other constituent organizations concerned with economic development practice and public development programs.

These audiences go well beyond the actors traditionally responsible for local economic development activities and the economic development planning and industrial development professionals who have traditionally staffed local development efforts. In many places, economic development is understood as industrial development—the process of attracting industries to increase the local rates of economic and employment growth. Local jurisdictions collectively employ thousands of industrial developers to engage in recruitment and promotional activities. As the supply of industrial sites and the scale of incentive packages grow relative to the demand for domestic facility locations sought by corporate entities, industrial recruitment and promotion are becoming less cost-effective. Industrial developers are exploring new development strategies to augment traditional industrial development efforts.

Economic development planners have engaged both in labor market analysis related to employment planning and skills training programs funded under the Comprehensive Employment and Training Act (CETA) or state vocational education programs and in economic development policy and program planning for cities, counties, and multi-county areas usually tied to the EDA or FmHA programs that offered grants for local infrastructure development. The federal funding for these programs has been reduced while other federal programs providing direct support for area-wide planning have been eliminated. Without adequate funding, local policy plans lack an operational base. Consequently economic development professionals are seeking new ways to become involved in the local economic development process. Thus both traditional and emerging participants in local economic development are working toward a more effective local economic development practice that is based on a fresh and open-minded consideration of the development process and on an awareness of the threats and opportunities emerging in U.S. localities.

In this book, I propose alternative roles and responsibilities for local actors based on a broad treatment of economic development. Industrial developers, economic development planners, employment specialists, and community developers may be able to increase their effectiveness and job security by considering the roles and responsibilities suggested in this book and embracing those that make sense for the organizations and areas with which they are affiliated. The scope of local economic development presented here includes industrial development, labor market analysis, area-wide policy planning, and other traditional economic development activities, yet goes beyond these areas of professional practice.

Like any book, this one makes many assumptions about the subject under discussion. The key assumptions are related to the threats and opportunities currently facing local actors concerned with economic development. The assumptions are as follows:

- Local actors will have more opportunity to play lead roles promoting economic development in the 1980s.
- Local actors will come under increasing pressure to achieve tangible results and to have visible, positive impacts on the local economic base.
- Local actors will have to improve the stature of the organizations with which they are affiliated to gain local credibility and acceptance as political pressures increase.
- Local actors will face more economic uncertainty and volatility in attempting to anticipate future economic change.
- Local actors will have to find new resources to deal with local economic problems.
- Local actors, individually, will not have much direct control over the local economy.

This book is written with these local actors in mind. Since more attention has been paid to urban/community economic development in declining central cities, the book recognizes the contexts of smaller communities and of the larger cities which face a variety of economic conditions including rapid economic growth, stability, or decline. Although a broad range of strategic and tactical alternatives is considered, emphasis is directed to the most innovative yet feasible approaches to promoting economic development.

For the book to be successful, it should help local actors gain critical insights and build skills that will increase their capacity to promote economic development. To formulate meaningful economic development strategies, local actors are provided a framework for understanding economic development. Assuming the perspective of the particular organizations with which they are affiliated, they are offered several modes of planning to identify and pursue meaningful roles and responsibilities. To participate in public-private partnerships, they are exposed to project planning and management and are shown how to relate local development strategies to local projects.

The book pays special attention to financing and economic feasibility in order to give local actors a better understanding of the business and banking perspectives relevant to public–private partnerships and co-development. While the treatment is introductory, it provides a solid analytical foundation by focusing on the basic principles of finance and marketing. The suggested readings, exercises, case studies, and appendixes reinforce the development of knowledge and analytical skills.

The book recognizes the growth of entrepreneurial activity in the public and nonprofit sectors. While such entrepreneurship should be encouraged, I stress the need for planning that defines clearly the public purposes and organizational objectives to be served as a basis for selecting the development activities in which to participate. To simply "do deals" will not do. The taxpayer's dollar is not well used when local projects are executed without a clear public purpose. Unless there is proper public planning, deal making becomes as vacuous as formulating economic development policies without the means to implement the recommendations. Thus, I support more flexible, developmental and active approaches to local economic development without ignoring the need to determine appropriate public purposes, strategies, and tactics.

Ultimately, the book has an ambitious goal. It seeks to promote public–private partnerships with an approach that balances strategy design and project execution on the one hand and socially responsible development and profitable local ventures on the other.

The books presents (1) how to understand better the local economic development process in Chapter 1, (2) how to design an effective planning process for local economic development in Chapter 2, (3) how to select an appropriate definition from alternative definitions of local economic development in Chapter 3, (4) how to devise and choose among particular business development strategies and effective tactics, and design meaningful roles for local economic development organizations in Chapter 3, (5) how to capitalize and manage a local business development fund in Chapter 4, (6) how to plan and manage economic development projects in Chapter 5, (7) how to structure financing for business development and real estate projects in Chapter 6, (8) how to do economic feasibility studies for real estate development and business development projects in Chapter 8, and (9) the national perspective on local development in Chapter 9. In Chapters 7 and 8, case examples are presented to reinforce the principles of financial analysis and market studies covered in Chapters 6 and 8, respectively.

The reader can use this book in several ways. For an overview of local economic development and finance, the reader should find Chapters 1 through 4 and 9 most useful. For an introduction to project planning, market and feasibility analysis, and project financing applied to local public–private development projects, Chapters 5 through 8 should be most relevant. To use the book more intensively as a text, the reader should work through the exercises and read the appendixes and selected references which are organized by topic in the bibliography as well as carefully read the chapters.

1

A PLANNING APPROACH
TO UNDERSTANDING
ECONOMIC DEVELOPMENT

Economic development became institutionalized after World War II as a formal field of study. Over the years, various theories and models have been proposed in an attempt to understand and promote the development of less-developed countries. Most studies of regional economic development in the United States are based on these theories and models. Unfortunately we have neither a single model of economic development nor a satisfactory theoretical explanation of the economic development process. The process is very complex. Countries industrialize and achieve higher levels of employment and material well-being. At the same time, unemployment, inequality, poverty, and political unrest often grow. Solutions to problems at an earlier stage of economic development often give rise to new problems during subsequent stages.

Two general models of economic development may be counterposed. Toward one extreme countries have withdrawn from the international economic order to become more self-reliant and to direct the construction of their national economic systems. Those with large internal markets or ample natural resources have achieved the most success. The autarkic period has been limited, however; at some point the countries seek to increase trade and import technology. Smaller countries have achieved far less through increased isolation and, in response, have sought the support of a major industrial power or have joined common markets.

Toward the other extreme countries have tried to expand and diversify their exports to realize the gains of international trade.

Free trade has been successful in particular countries during particular periods. However, failures have also occurred as reflected in deteriorating economic conditions, burdensome foreign debt, and dependence on external sources of aid.

Associated with the first model are the concepts of the planned economy and local self-reliance. Yet the realities of inefficiency, slow growth, and low incomes have overshadowed the rhetoric of these ideas. With the second model comes the belief in the efficacy of free enterprise as embodied in the national and multinational corporation. In reality, this institution has not proved powerful enough to increase economic growth and distributive justice simultaneously.

The international development experience warns against the acceptance of any narrow development doctrine or the dogmatic application of any set of development policies. The framework suggested below avoids dichotomous and extreme positions. Instead of choosing between market or planned solutions, we must seek ways to achieve jointly more coordination and more competition, greater productivity with greater fairness, and increased innovation supported by improved guidance systems.

Economic development models and the theories to be discussed in Chapter 3 weigh the importance of intentional human activity quite differently. To some theorists economic development is a process that happens; there are structural forces—technical, social, and market—that create the dynamic that drives the economic development process. Although people generate development through productive activity, the causal forces of development are to be understood without reference to specific actions or particular individuals. These theorists consider the verb, to develop, to be intransitive. Other theorists suggest that the process does not occur so deterministically. Individuals acting to derive sustenance from their environment constitute the essential dynamic that drives the economic development process. People cause economic development to happen when they bring something latent into activity or make an idea something real. In this sense the verb is transitive (Arndt 1981).

In this book economic development is viewed as a process involving people purposively doing productive things. In other words, "to develop" is understood in its transitive sense. We can and do pursue our intentions, although we cannot change the world in any way we please. We can act more effectively to promote economic development with knowledge of three mutually reinforcing constructs: a conceptual framework, a strategic perspective, and a theory of economic development. The framework is presented in the next section. The other two constructs are articulated in the next two chapters.

ORGANIZATIONAL PLANNING FRAMEWORK

For human beings, power is our ability to do work. At the most elementary level, economic development is the product of work—various forms of purposive human activity through which we derive sustenance from our environment. Work is structured into the tasks of production, management, and planning.

Production: Most people *do* work. For example, a construction worker helps build a factory; an operative assembles electrical components; a secretary types a letter.

Management: Some people *direct* those who do work. A foreman supervises construction or production activities; an administrator discusses program goals with her staff; a manager puts together next year's budget.

Planning: Fewer people *plan* work. A company president outlines the basic elements of a new expansion strategy; top managers examine alternative ways to redeploy their company's assets to achieve higher profitability; a businessman meets with his backers to present a plan to start a new franchise operation.

Obviously, these forms of work are all necessary and interdependent. Still, planning work is the most essential type of work. Because we must accept the results of decisions made in the past and make decisions in a complex and changing present, we must plan work in order to face the realities of an uncertain future. As Professor Frank Knight said about 70 years ago:

> With uncertainty present, doing things, the actual execution of activity, becomes in a real sense a secondary part of life; the primary problem or function is deciding what to do and how to do it. (Knight 1971, p. 268)

This argument is very helpful in gaining an understanding of economic development. People who plan work, pursuing their ends by applying available means, are ultimately responsible for the changes in the political economy. They use their power to decide what to produce, how to produce, when and where to produce, and by whom the production will be done. At the local level, the planning of economic development results in changes in the economic base of the area.

From an organizational perspective, business start-ups, expansions, contractions, and bankruptcies, when augmented by public investments, determine the changes in the local economy. The success of a particular plan is related to the power expended by the organization to execute the plan, which ultimately depends upon organizational resources and the power expended by other organizations to execute their plans. The execution of organizational plans continually impacts upon and modifies the local environment.

In an advanced economy like that of the United States, most people plan, manage, or perform work in and through such organizations, which range from the largest private or public employers and corporate giants to the multitude of small corporations, partnerships, sole proprietorships, nonprofit organizations, and public agencies. People in these organizations produce different things (20–30 million products in the U.S. economy alone).

Obviously, this organizational network is very complex, but the most important questions can be identified by applying the organizational framework sketched above. How powerful is the organization? Can it successfully carry out its plans? Who controls the organization? Are these persons local or nonlocal planners? In addition to examining the dynamics of existing business entities, we must examine organizational births and learn who is creating new businesses, how and for what purposes. Although answers to these questions do not constitute a *theory* of economic development, they do offer a *framework* for applying any particular economic development theory.

From the perspective of local leaders designing economic development organizations and local professionals staffing such organizations, three environments are relevant: the environment that is internal to the organization, the external environment that corresponds to the local area, and the nonlocal external environment. Three sets of organizations exist: the local economic development organization, all other local organizations, and all other nonlocal organizations. Even in a small community, many organizations will usually influence the local economy. Although some are more powerful than others, these organizations function as a network of peer organizations—an "interorganization." The economic development process embodies reciprocal relationships between organizations adapting to changing environments and environments adopting productive activity directed by and through organizations.

In the interorganization, the planning of work is not well coordinated. Planners pursue different aims and intentions and have imperfect knowledge of their environments. Furthermore, our economic system encourages competition among these organizations. Central direction and collusive practices receive little support. Not surprisingly, then, plans are not often realized as they are intended. The difference between realization and intention does not result from people failing to plan or act rationally, for planners do pursue means that would best achieve desired organizational ends. Rather, because each organization plans independently of other organizations, everyone's intentions are likely to be frustrated, at least in part. As inconsistent and incompatible plans are executed, things simply go wrong. This is an accurate way of portraying the environmental complexity and uncertainty faced by local planners. Thus, limited and imperfect information about the external environment is equivalent to ignorance of the intentions, resources, and actions of other organizations. (See Exercise 1.)

COMPARISONS TO PRIVATE AND PUBLIC INVESTMENT PLANNING

Subsequent chapters will present views on the planning and management of local economic development. To provide a backdrop for these discussions, we briefly consider the typical kind of planning conducted by large corporations, small businesses, and government entities. As noted above, the major impetus for investment planning is uncertainty. If the world were certain, we could concentrate on doing what was necessary. In an uncertain world, we must plan what to do and how to do it.

Investment planning determines the content and structure of the production process which, in turn, determines the levels and types of employment and output. Large national and multinational corporations account for most of the "gross domestic private investment." Smaller businesses and other private organizations account for the rest. Federal, state, and local governments, government districts, public authorities and other public organizations are responsible for public investment, although the amounts are often not distinguished in the figures on government expenditures.

The corporate investment planner knows that the company must remain dynamic and adaptable so as not to lose ground to competitors. The investment criteria of expected return and anticipated risk are further specified and shaped by internal corporate policies and external economic conditions. Investment planning determines the form, amount, timing, and location of corporate investments. Some common forms of investment include expansion of existing facilities, investment in new branch plants, acquisition of or merger with other companies, purchase or sale of securities, real estate or currency, closure of existing facilities, acquisition of young growing companies, or investment in new ventures.

When a large corporation decides to undertake an investment project, the matter is simple from an administrative and management point of view. As a going concern, the company has structures and functions in place that provide support. The design, financing, and execution of the project are normally controlled from within the corporation. A management team with experience in planning and implementing the particular type of project is assembled. The administrative capacity usually exists to carry out new projects, even multimillion dollar and multiyear efforts. Corporate management may also hire outside consultants, borrow capital from financial intermediaries, or raise debt and equity capital in the public markets to implement investment plans.

In contrast, the investment planning of smaller companies is much more limited in scope. Larger companies tend to expand or reduce existing productive capacity, but smaller companies are more likely to start or close their businesses. Compared to larger companies, smaller companies have less control of the external economic environment and usually assume more risk to achieve their objectives. They must locate a niche in the market, find sufficient equity capital, debt capital, or both, and have the good fortune to avoid fatal events such as a sudden downturn in the local economy, an escalation of interest rates or costs of key inputs, evaporation of capital sources, or severe delays in construction, operations, accounts receivable, or government approvals. Although most smaller companies seek to grow and remain independent, survival is never assured. Most survivors remain small, marginal companies; only the most innovative prosper. The most successful become large companies.

Small business development is executed by two different types of individuals. The overwhelming majority of small businesses are started by persons with limited business experience, inadequate capital, or weak management skills. In some instances they have become self-employed for lack of an alternative source of employment. While seeking the rewards of self-employment, most show up in the statistics of small-business failures.

The remaining minority of small businesses are begun by persons who have resigned from corporate positions to strike out on their own, forfeiting job security for the chance to make large capital gains. They are drawn from the ranks of corporate executives, managers, and technicians who have had extensive involvement in a particular line of work or area of business. They have developed an idea from their work experience that could lead to a potentially profitable and manageable enterprise. They turn to business associates, venture capitalists, or investment bankers for the financial and organizational support required to initiate new ventures. Although failure rates are high, such successful young businesses tend to become the fastest growing and most technologically advanced companies in the economy.

Public investment planning proceeds very differently. The investment criteria are satisfaction of public wants and needs and fulfillment of statutory responsibilities. The constraints are set by the local economic base and the limits of the power to tax, spend, regulate, and control. Rather than initiating profitable ventures, local public investments provide public goods and services—schools and other public buildings, roads, water and sewer lines, etc. The legal foundations for the typical public investment are fairly clear. The public decision-making process, which includes budget proposals, public hearings and referenda, and financing from the sale of government bonds, is well established. Local government managers, finance officers, planners, and attorneys have experience in executing various capital improvement projects.

Economic development planning that is typically pursued at the local level shares common ground with each of these types of investment planning. Like public investment planning, economic development planning is intended to improve the wellbeing of the people living in a particular geographic area, usually a political jurisdiction. Priority should be given to the economic development projects that best meet local social objectives. Like private investment planning, economic development planning must consider the private returns and anticipated risks to private developers and business executives of potential public–private economic development projects. Like small-business investment plans, economic development projects tend to be locally controlled and relatively small-scale in terms of cost, duration, and results.

The organizational planning framework poses generic distinctions between organizations in terms of their power, plans, and purposes, which are more important than their status as public or private organizations. Local actors affiliated with private for-profit, nonprofit, and public organizations are all important participants in the local economic development process.

Local public officials and professionals responsible for economic development typically have limited resources and power relative to the potential scope and scale of effort. Therefore they can accomplish more tasks by working with and through other local organizations, the network of peer organizations that are locally based. They must inspire, support, facilitate, and sometimes challenge action on the part of others. They must know and be comfortable with the key actors of the local interorganization.

2

MODES OF PLANNING ECONOMIC DEVELOPMENT

Planning economic development is an activity most closely identified with the developing countries that prepare national economic plans and development budgets and pursue large-scale public investment projects. There are few parallel U.S. experiences. The National Resources Planning Board engaged in economic planning but without implementation authority and for only a limited time during the New Deal. The Tennessee Valley Authority prepared comprehensive regional development plans during its early history but narrowed its focus to public power production thereafter. The idea of national or regional economic planning has reared its head occasionally since 1950, usually corresponding in timing and intensity to the downturns of the business cycle. On the other hand, local U.S. planning institutions are well established although traditionally focused on the planning and management of physical development.

Practically every domestic assistance program created by the federal government since 1950 has required the preparation of local plans as prerequisites to accessing federal funds and other program resources. A plethora of local plans has been developed for human services, employment training, low-income housing, transportation, environmental quality, water resources, etc. The economic development programs were not excepted. Economic development plans were prepared in development districts and larger planning regions for the EDA. More recently, EDA proposed the Comprehensive Economic Development Strategy which stressed planning for the execution of economic development projects that were related to local economic development policies (Friedman 1979).

As the federal government reduces domestic assistance, local planning to meet federal requirements declines. Replacing requirements planning is planning that responds to local initiatives and interests. This orientation returns local planning to its pre–World War II status.

In this chapter, we are concerned with designing a local economic development planning process that is relevant to U.S. localities in terms of the problems and opportunities that they are facing during the 1980s. The aim is to present two modes of normative planning that can accommodate and enhance local initiatives, public–private partnerships, and co-development efforts. These normative modes combine general principles of planning and link them to specific planning contexts and planning situations (Galloway 1979 and Kaufman 1979). They are called contingency planning and strategic planning.

Contingency and strategic planning are best understood in comparison to synoptic-comprehensive planning. Although often criticized, the latter remains the standard or, at least, the point of departure for normative discussions of the local planning process. Bendavid-Val 1980 has made a contribution by specifying and applying the synoptic-comprehensive model to local economic development in the U.S. context. He argues that local planning should follow sequential steps which should be linked to create a continuous planning process: analyzing data, defining community goals and objectives, designing alternative courses of action, assessing and comparing alternatives, selecting the preferred alternative, and implementing and evaluating the chosen alternative.

As shown in Table 1, synoptic-comprehensive planning is areawide planning; the entire community is the subject of planning. It is consumer oriented because it seeks to satisfy local needs that reflect the public interest. The product of planning may be visualized as an overlay that prescribes the actions required for successful implementation.

Contingency and strategic planning are forms of organizational planning vested in local development organizations (LDOs). They are producer oriented to the extent that the aims, resources, and capabilities of the LDO are determined first, before areawide goals and problems are addressed. Rather than representing a general prescriptive plan for all local organizations, the plan of the LDO is but one piece in the mosaic of organizational plans which must be jointly executed.

TABLE 1. Modes of Planning

Features of planning	Synoptic-comprehensive planning	Contingency and strategic planning
Subject	Community as a whole	Local development organizations
Goals	Achieving the public interest or social welfare function	Achieving organizational goals compatible with community goals
Orientation	Consumer-oriented: achieve goals to satisfy local needs	Producer-oriented: define organizational capabilities to attack local problems
Nature of product	Prescriptive overlay	Mosaic of organizational plans
Action emphasis	Desirable alternatives	Feasible alternatives
Inspiration	National planning	Corporate planning

Source: Compiled by author.

Certainly areawide planning is needed. Synoptic-comprehensive planning can help identify key actors, articulate shared goals, mobilize scarce local resources, and surface local conflicts. However, the realities of planning for local economic development caution against making synoptic-comprehensive planning the primary focus of local planning efforts. Local planners require better rudders and anchors to pursue economic development successfully. Contingency and strategic planning hold more promise particularly in the following situations: when meaningful goals are difficult to define, value conflicts among contentious interests prevent agreement on important policies, planning resources are meager, fragmented, or difficult to coordinate, and the community expects tangible actions and concrete results.

Local officials and leaders designing the organizational arrangements for local economic development planning should seriously consider the proper organization or agency to be vested with the lead role, the organization's director, and in larger communities, the organization's staffing. Planning at the organizational level should be encouraged and initially given priority. The practice of local economic development is sufficiently broad to support areawide planning that is compatible with organizational planning. Moreover, areawide planning should become more effective as a result.

LDO directors and staff should use contingency and strategic planning to put together plans for their *own* organization and then lead efforts to plan for the community as a whole. With organizational planning providing the structure for areawide planning, LDOs are in the best position to establish local economic development strategies that overcome goal and value conflicts, resource constraints, and disagreements surrounding particular projects. With contingency plans or strategic plans providing the base, the LDO will be in a much better position to play its appropriate role in promoting local economic development with and through other organizations.

Contingency planning is recommended for local executives who are directing an organization with very limited economic development experience, few resources, scarcely any professional staff, and one that is under great pressure to show results. As resources and experience are gained, it should be attractive to undertake strategic planning. In the long term, strategic planning and contingency planning, woven together, create a sound basis for planning local economic development from the perspective of the LDO.

The following descriptions of contingency and strategic planning are written for the executive directors who have the lead role in local economic development planning, as well as for the local officials, members of advisory bodies, and professionals staffing LDOs. For simplicity, the local actor leading these planning activities is referred to as "the planner."

CONTINGENCY PLANNING

This formulation of contingency planning is aimed at increasing the local development organization's credibility and effectiveness in promoting local economic development. In contrast to strategic planning which, to be treated seriously, requires heavier time and resource commitments, contingency planning aims at achieving concrete results with less time and fewer resources.

Contingency planning for local economic development is conditional planning. Instead of forecasting future events, future events are anticipated without regard to exactly when they might occur.

Rather than setting goals and objectives at the outset of the planning process, contingency planning avoids potential goal conflicts by focusing on responses to specific events. Rather than generating options and alternatives to address general goals or conditions, mitigation plans and project plans are designed with specific contingencies in mind.

Contingency planning offers a balanced treatment of analysis, design, and implementation. It may be divided into six steps: (1) identifying contingencies, (2) screening identified contingencies, (3) constructing indicators of contingencies and specifying trigger points, (4) designing first-cut responses to contingencies, (5) formulating contingency plan(s), and (6) implementing contingency plan(s). The first three steps are primarily analytical. Steps 4 and 5 are dominated by design considerations. The final step focuses on implementation. An overview is provided in Figure 1.

Identifying Contingencies

Experienced local planners should understand the political economy well enough to anticipate the potential economic changes that would affect the community. Yet they may not be able to predict with any accuracy either the timing of those changes or which changes might occur within any given time frame. Of course, contingent events will vary with the social, economic, political, and geographic profile of the community and will reflect the scope of the local economic planning function. In the United States, local planners would typically consider contingent events such as the introduction of a new branch plant, the development of a competitive suburban shopping mall, proposals for large-scale energy exploitation projects, the rapid influx of population, successful unionization drives, the closing of a local plant or military installation, significant shifts in national economic policies, the depletion of important local natural resources, and other important economic events.

Notice that contingency planning does not begin with the identification, formulation, or prioritization of goals and objectives. Rather, the planner focuses on the external environment and identifies contingent events that would have major economic impacts on local employment, income, tax revenues, prices, and property values. Moreover, contingent events would not include natural disasters or

FIG. 1. Contingency-Planning Flow Chart

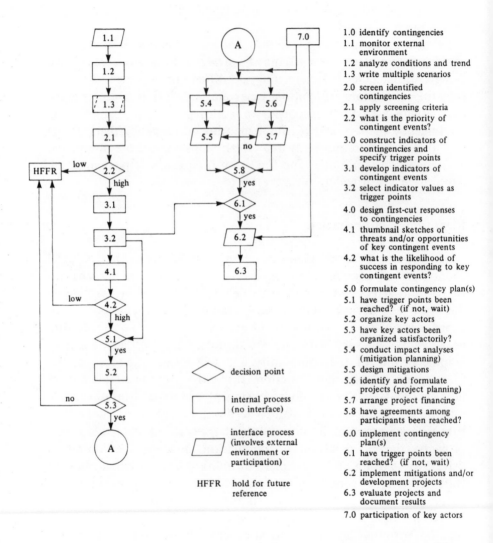

1.0 identify contingencies
1.1 monitor external environment
1.2 analyze conditions and trend
1.3 write multiple scenarios

2.0 screen identified contingencies
2.1 apply screening criteria
2.2 what is the priority of contingent events?

3.0 construct indicators of contingencies and specify trigger points
3.1 develop indicators of contingent events
3.2 select indicator values as trigger points

4.0 design first-cut responses to contingencies
4.1 thumbnail sketches of threats and/or opportunities of key contingent events
4.2 what is the likelihood of success in responding to key contingent events?

5.0 formulate contingency plan(s)
5.1 have trigger points been reached? (if not, wait)
5.2 organize key actors
5.3 have key actors been organized satisfactorily?
5.4 conduct impact analyses (mitigation planning)
5.5 design mitigations
5.6 identify and formulate projects (project planning)
5.7 arrange project financing
5.8 have agreements among participants been reached?

6.0 implement contingency plan(s)
6.1 have trigger points been reached? (if not, wait)
6.2 implement mitigations and/or development projects
6.3 evaluate projects and document results

7.0 participation of key actors

Reprinted with permission from Malizia, "Contingency Planning for Local Economic Development," in *Environment and Planning B*, vol. 9 (June 1982), pp. 163–176.

random events that would cause local emergencies but for which special channels of response were already established. The insurance and security functions, while imperfect, have been institutionalized to deal with such contingencies.

Because of the importance of this first step of contingency planning, regular monitoring should be established. To avoid elaborate and costly information systems, efforts should be targeted and remain alert to corporate and government decisions that could affect the local economy dramatically. The periodic reports of any corporation that employs more than five percent of the local work force should be read. Sharing information with local economic development planners in other communities where these companies have other facilities is strongly recommended.

We have no set methodology for identifying contingent events, although methods drawn from "futures research" are suggestive. Whatever method we use, we must take care to identify a manageable number of contingent events.

Screening Identified Contingencies

In the second step of contingency planning, contingent events are divided into one category that receives further attention and another that receives no further attention. By applying three specific criteria, the planner should seek to screen out enough of the identified contingencies to make the third and fourth steps described below manageable. The criteria are importance, imminence, and pressure.

The criterion of importance gauges economic impacts, that is, the quantity, income, price, and wealth effects of contingent events in terms of benefits and costs.[1] Important contingent events also impact upon the local quality of life—the quality of the workplace environment, the quality of the natural environment, long-term community stability, local amenities, etc. In addition to objective impacts, the planner should be sensitive to subjective factors which give symbolic importance to contingent events, and to local political and economic interests affected by them.

Imminence is the probability that a contingent event will occur in the near term (say, one to three years). In a turbulent environment, these probabilities need only be discriminating enough to rank-order contingencies or at least place them in "more likely" and "less likely" categories. Using imminence and importance in combination, the planner will know the most significant contingent events.

Unlike these criteria which refer to the external economic environment, pressure refers to the response time and staff resources that are needed to address a contingent event adequately. The longer the necessary lead time or the more resources required, the greater the pressure. Imminent contingent events will bestow shorter lead times but may not overly tax planning resources. Important contingent events will usually be more taxing but may evolve slowly enough to create little pressure.

Constructing Indicators and Specifying Trigger Points

The next step is to decide how to monitor key contingencies and when to respond to them. Qualitative indicators will be useful as long as they are readily comprehensible. Quantitative indicators will be useful as long as values for trigger points are easily set. Indicators should be straightforward and easy to interpret, based upon widely available information or information that is not expensive to collect, and easy to construct in the form of rates, ratios, or percentages.

For indicators of each contingent event, values must be set that will serve as triggers for both detailed planning and for each stage of implementation. For example, detailed planning may begin when a company announces plans to locate in the community. The triggers for executing plans may be tied to the initiation of facility construction. As noted, the local planner will not be concerned with when, in real time, actions shall be taken. Rather, the planner will want to act in time to deal with the contingent event.

Design First-Cut Responses

First-cut responses outline the scope and sequence of actions proposed to address key contingent events. The most basic requirement of this step is to view each contingent event as both a *threat* and an *opportunity*. This duality is present in all contingencies, although one aspect is often more dominant.[2] The emphasis on dual treatment of contingent events is necessary to compensate for the one-sided treatment that contingency planning has received in corporate and military planning. In these applications, contingency planning is oriented to minimizing the negative effects of threats that would occur if a turbulent environment were to upset projections and basic assumptions of the strategic plan or if a competitor (adversary) were to take an unexpected action.

Logically, first-cut responses fall into one of four categories. The response may be to do nothing significant, to mitigate threats only, to seize opportunities only, or to respond to both threats and opportunities. In deciding how far to take any series of responses, the planner must weigh the level of required effort (resource requirements) against the likelihood of success in achieving the intended results. In making this determination, we may be able to weed out contingencies that require too much effort relative to potential results.

First-cut responses lay out the critical threats and opportunities of contingencies. To lay out the overall design, a series of conditional (if–then) statements for each contingent event should be outlined.

It is preferable to develop first-cut responses without attracting public attention. The public may not fully understand that trying to anticipate contingent events is not the same as predicting events, or that effective responses are often difficult to find once contingencies have been identified. For this reason, assuming a low profile avoids unnecessary explanations or misunderstandings. On the other hand, the final two steps of contingency planning require active public participation.

Formulating Contingency Plan(s)

The first task of this step is to organize key actors. Based on first-cut responses, the planner should be able to identify the actors whose participation and support are essential to bring about the desired results. These actors or their designated representatives must be brought together to initiate detailed planning. If key actors cannot be mobilized around a contingent event, contingency planning should proceed no further.

Detailed planning should begin for each contingent event around which there is organized interest and support. Paralleling the duality of threat and opportunity, the planning process should be divided into *mitigation* planning and *project* planning. Mitigation planning involves making estimates of the probable magnitude of impacts from contingent events, proposing ways to minimize these negative impacts, and forging agreements needed to carry out these proposals. Techniques from economic, fiscal, and environmental impact analysis should be useful for estimating negative effects. Implementation procedures may be embodied in consensus resolutions, formal agreements, or informal agreements, depending upon legal requirements and the number and preferences of the participants involved.

In project planning, unlike mitigation planning, which is primarily reactive, the planner attempts to seize the opportunities afforded by each contingent event. Four activities, in addition to organization of key actors, should be emphasized as part of the project planning and management cycle: project identification, formulation, financing, and evaluation. As with mitigation planning, a set of agreements among participants is needed for successful implementation. Project planning is discussed more fully in Chapter 5.

In planning for local economic development, we may not need to develop formal contingency plans. Instead, ideas may be presented to key actors, and the creative mitigations or projects that are suggested may be recorded in any understandable form. The responses should be fleshed out in sufficient detail to see the entire sequence of actions and to give each actor an idea of the scope and timing of his or her responsibilities. The detailed designs should be translated into a set of agreements among participants that serve as a work plan.

Implementing Contingency Plan(s)

Local planners use the agreements reached during mitigation planning and project planning to facilitate implementation. They usually have to remind key actors of responsibilities and commitments, do liaison work to help coordinate various actors, troubleshoot to prevent breakdowns and to minimize bottlenecks, and periodically assess progress. As unforseen problems arise, they attempt to forge revised agreements, suggest additional designs, or involve new actors. In short, the planner endeavors to get the job done in spite of Murphy's Law.

As noted above in Step 3, the implementation of each contingency plan is keyed to the trigger points of selected indicators.

Very little technical guidance can be given on implementation in general terms. In local economic development planning, the political bargaining will be intense when jobs, contracts, profits, bank deposits, and capital gains or losses are at stake. The local planner will need a good deal of skill, experience, and good luck to achieve success. Successful implementation will depend mainly on the commitment of lead actors, the working consensus among them, the resources contributed by key organizations, the coordination among organizations, and the extent of local public support.

The local planner needs to demonstrate that planning can lead to desirable outcomes and can achieve tangible results. Thus, the planner must document the results of contingency planning, find out which mitigations achieved their intended purposes, track projects that were successfully carried out, and report outcomes in terms of their positive impacts on the community. Contingency planning is more fully explained by Linneman (1980), Linneman and Chandran (1981), Malizia (1982), and O'Connor (1978). For an example of contingency planning cast in a local economic development context, see Malizia (1982).

STRATEGIC PLANNING

The most important thing to remember when doing strategic planning is that the planner is planning for his or her particular local development organization. The planner should hold fast to this organizational focus, notwithstanding the fact that the ultimate concern is with promoting economic development in the locality on an area-wide basis. The organization represents ground zero, the origin from which the planner formulates an approach to local economic development. Too often the local planner tries to plan for the community at large or for a committee of local actors representing different local peer organizations. These resulting plans are usually very general and somewhat inconsistent. They often lack substantial local support or serious resource commitments. More problematically, the local planner preparing such plans is diverted from doing organizational planning. Such organizational planning should provide a rudder for guiding broader-based local economic development efforts. Furthermore, the local planner cannot assume that devising general plans or writing up broad policy statements provides good currency for increasing local credibility and support. This currency is already declining and may be devalued severely in the years ahead.

Like contingency planning, strategic planning embraces analysis, design, and implementation tasks. It may be divided into five steps:

FIG. 2. Strategic Planning Flow Chart

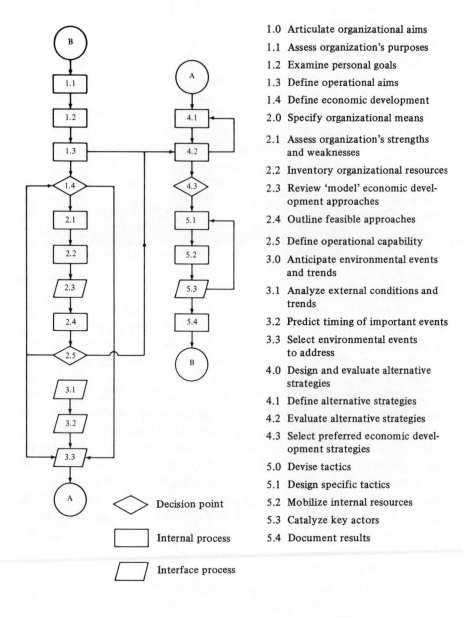

1.0 Articulate organizational aims

1.1 Assess organization's purposes

1.2 Examine personal goals

1.3 Define operational aims

1.4 Define economic development

2.0 Specify organizational means

2.1 Assess organization's strengths and weaknesses

2.2 Inventory organizational resources

2.3 Review 'model' economic development approaches

2.4 Outline feasible approaches

2.5 Define operational capability

3.0 Anticipate environmental events and trends

3.1 Analyze external conditions and trends

3.2 Predict timing of important events

3.3 Select environmental events to address

4.0 Design and evaluate alternative strategies

4.1 Define alternative strategies

4.2 Evaluate alternative strategies

4.3 Select preferred economic development strategies

5.0 Devise tactics

5.1 Design specific tactics

5.2 Mobilize internal resources

5.3 Catalyze key actors

5.4 Document results

◇ Decision point

▭ Internal process

▱ Interface process

26

(1) articulating organizational aims, (2) specifying organizational means, (3) anticipating environmental events and trends, (4) designing and evaluating alternative strategies, and (5) devising tactics for executing desired strategy. An overview of strategic planning is given in Figure 2.

Articulating Organizational Aims

To have a grounding for planning local economic development, the local planner should ask, what are the overriding aims of this organization? A community development director answered this question, as follows: to secure adequate funding to continue the community development staff at their current level of effort. The executive director of a local Chamber of Commerce receiving city funds to promote economic development answered it this way: to be recognized by public officials as a fair and effective organization while maintaining the support of the local business community. An industrial developer had the narrow aim of selling an available industrial site to a national corporation. A city manager wanted to convince the mayor to dissolve the existing administrative arrangements and vest his office with responsibility for promoting local economic development. As these examples suggest, the local planner should answer this question as honestly as possible and answer it privately or in the company of trusted staff members.

The next question is, how can promoting local economic development serve these aims or purposes? By answering this question, the local planner may begin to consider economic development from the perspective of the opportunities afforded her or his organization. He or she has to sketch out various economic development outcomes that help achieve organizational aims. These sketches should lead to the next question: Which local economic development problems should be tackled? Which have to be addressed? Responses to these questions describe the orientation and position that the local development organization will seek when dealing with local economic development.

Finally, the planner should consider which definition of local economic development is most compatible with the answers given to all of the above questions. A definition should be formulated that is compatible with the idea of doing good in the local community as well as doing well for the local development organization.

Specifying Organizational Means

With this step the local planner shifts the focus on the internal environment from organizational goals to organizational resources. Again, the planner must conduct an honest assessment of the organization's strengths and weaknesses: What do we do best? What have we done poorly? Which activities have given us status and recognition in the past? When have we gotten mud on our faces and why?

Upon completion of a frank assessment of strengths and weaknesses, inventories of staff, budget, and other organizational resources should be undertaken and linked to the organization's basic capabilities. At this stage, the planner outlines a few general approaches to promoting local economic development, as was done in the previous step, that exploit the organization's strengths and effectively utilize its resource base. The planner should also examine model approaches to local economic development that have been successfully applied elsewhere in relation to the legal and political constraints operating locally. This examination should lead to a narrowing and sharpening of alternatives to ones that are feasible in terms of the organization's capabilities, legal constraints, political realities, and external forms of support. This analysis will frequently require modification of the tentative definition of local economic development posed in Step 1.

Anticipating Environmental Events and Trends

The local planner moves from consideration of the internal environment of the organization to an analysis of the external environment. The longer the time frame for strategic planning, the more difficult the analysis and the more general the results. Long-term planning requires attention to the technological, social, political, and market forces that will affect the local economy. The recommendation here is to focus on shorter-term economic trends and try to anticipate the environmental events that may occur and have significant impacts on the local economy over the next few years.

The process of anticipating environmental events is very similar to anticipating contingent events, as described in the last section. The major difference is that the timing of environmental events must be forecasted in strategic planning in addition to determining whether they are likely to occur.

The planner next examines each environmental event relative to the organization's aims and capabilities. The examination should conclude with the decision either to gear up activities to confront the environmental event or to ignore it. This step completes the analysis phase of strategic planning.

Designing and Evaluating Alternative Strategies

Designing and evaluating alternative strategies are the most creative and innovative aspects of strategic planning. Strategy is "the general's art." It is the game plan or the different paths for achieving organizational aims. With the results of the analysis phase in hand, the planner should be able to describe what actions to take to achieve organizational aims. To fashion the best strategy, alternatives should be designed and evaluated in an interactive process. Strategies are usually more general than the mitigations or projects identified under contingency planning. In fact, strategic courses of action can be used to frame and guide the design of specific mitigations or projects. No single method is adequate for designing strategic alternatives; however, useful techniques are presented in the next section of this chapter.

Distinguishing between what the local development organization must do and what other organizations must do to execute any strategy successfully is extremely important. Resources must be allocated both to activities over which the planner has control and to activities required for supporting, enticing, and cajoling others to act compatibly. In the environment of peer organizations, failure to determine how best to motivate others is the easiest way to turn a strategy into an empty wish.

When the preferred strategies are developed, the planner should return to the definition of local economic development and revise it, if necessary, in a way that is consistent with the chosen strategies. Like the best strategies, the most appropriate definition of local economic development is one that both increases the chances of achieving organizational aims and contributes to improving the local economy.

Devising Tactics

To carry out any desired strategy, the local planner should use a variety of management control tools which are helpful in project execution and policy or program implementation. The basic question is, how is the organization going to initiate, sustain, and complete preferred strategies? To answer this question, the planner needs to decide who is going to do what and when. The planner may use a work plan format in which tasks and subtasks are listed and charted over time intervals, usually months. The work plan helps keep track of critical stages, project milestones, decision points, and patterns of resource utilization.

As with contingency planning, the planner should identify key actors, forge agreements among them, and try to anticipate the many things that could go wrong. What should be done if things start falling apart? What are the second-best alternatives? Are there ways to save face? What can be learned when failure is inevitable? The planner must carefully consider when to terminate efforts and accept defeat or, conversely, when to declare a victory.

Efforts should be documented carefully whether they are successful or unsuccessful. This material will be vital to learn how to improve strategic planning in the next round. If success is achieved, the material should also be used to make others aware of the organization's accomplishments.

In both strategic and contingency planning, implementation is a crucial part of the process. If an environmental or contingent event occurred, a planner could not justify the prior steps of strategic or contingency planning without taking the concrete actions embodied in the last step. Community support for economic development planning will not depend upon the excellence of planning procedures but on the visible, beneficial results achieved.

Three additional rules of thumb should improve strategic planning:

● Keep it simple (a project with seven sequential tasks, each having a 90 percent chance of successful completion, has less than a 50–50 chance of being finished).
● Distinguish the essential from the preferred.
● Be modest about organizational aims, resources, and capabilities.

For additional discussion of strategic planning, see Drucker (1974), Levin (1981), and Steiner (1979). For examples in a local development context, see Hirschhorn (1980), and the business development strategies presented in the next chapter.

DESIGN AND ANALYSIS TECHNIQUES

The identification of environmental events in strategic planning and contingent events in contingency planning, the formulation of effective responses or new projects, and the analysis of impacts and results are important steps under both modes of planning. The techniques reviewed briefly here can help the local planner generate first-cut strategies or contingency plans without excessive resource or time commitments. The design techniques are *brainstorming* and *scenario writing*. The analysis techniques are *economic base, input–output,* and *shift–share* analysis. With respect to the interaction between the organization and its external environment, design techniques help develop ways that an organization can influence its environment; analysis techniques help gauge the environment's impact on the organization.

The first-cut planning process involves the following steps: Identify a few environmental/contingent events, assess the major impacts on the local economy, select the key event, design responses to this event, present the different results of these responses. Brainstorming is useful at every step except selection. Brainstorming is based on the following rules: Free-associate; defer judgment; do not evaluate your ideas. Seek quantity; list as many items as possible. Look for combinations and permutations of your ideas.

Scenario writing is a description of a process that may unfold, but it is written as if the process had already happened. Thus, a scenario is written in the past tense about possible future events, impacts, responses, and results as shown in Figure 3. A scenario should be plausible, consistent, and process oriented. The planner should be able to express his or her implicit understanding of what may take place. (See Exercise 2.)

In the practice of corporate planning, scenario writing is intimately related to both strategic planning and contingency planning. The strategic corporate plan is based upon the most likely scenario evolving over the long term. Contingency plans address one or more shorter-term, pessimistic scenarios. See O'Connor (1978), Hirschhorn (1980), and Linstone and Simmons (1977).

Economic base, input–output, and shift–share analyses are well-known techniques for economic forecasting and economic impact analysis. In an economic base study, one calculates an export-base

FIG. 3. Scenario-Writing Perspective

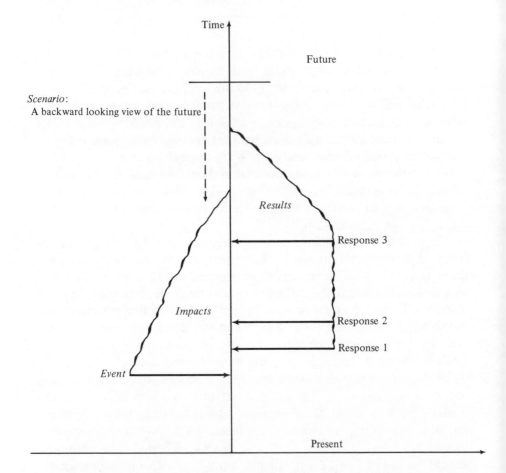

multiplier that may be used to predict the local results derived from a change in external demand for local exports (see Shah 1979). Input–output models also rely upon multipliers to predict the local output, income, or employment changes generated by changes in "final demand" (see Richardson 1972). Shift–share analysis is a tool for decomposing temporal changes in local output or employment, either historical or predicted, into components related to national growth, industrial mix, or local share (see Stevens and Moore 1980). These techniques with examples of their application and exercises are explained more fully in Bendavid-Val (1983), Czamanski (1972), and Isard (1960).

The analytical techniques may be used without reference to the theories of economic development that partly justify and support their application. Yet they become richer and more powerful when grounded in their proper theoretical contexts, which are presented in the next chapter. Economic base analysis grows directly out of economic base theory. The input–output model, which is used to do input–output analysis, is presented as an extension and elaboration of the economic base model. Input–output can also be used to suggest the relevance of changes in industrial mix to economic development. Product cycle theory relates regional industry changes to phases of the product cycle and provides a grounding for the application of shift–share analysis.

NOTES

1. Economic impacts may be usefully categorized as quantity effects, income effects, price effects, and wealth effects. Quantity effects include changes in output, employment, and other inputs; income effects cover changes in all sources of income—wages and salaries, rents, profits, and other property income. Price effects refer to changes in relative prices of local commodities such as food prices, rent levels, and wage rates. Wealth effects include the capital appreciation or depreciation of land values, facility values, inventory values, and the values of other assets as realized through capital gains and losses.

2. The Chinese ideogram for the word "crisis" is instructive in this regard. There are two characters: wei and chi. The first means danger; the second means opportunity.

3

THE SUBSTANCE OF LOCAL ECONOMIC DEVELOPMENT

Ideally, the local actors should be able to promote economic development by drawing from a solid understanding of the economic development process. However, we have no consensus explanation of economic development. Rather, explanations compete and conflict. This situation poses both threats and opportunities for local actors. On the one hand, ambiguity and the lack of understanding could lead to misguided strategies and the failure to recognize feasible alternatives. On the other hand, an opportunity exists to shape the understanding of economic development held by local citizens and leaders in ways that increase the local development organization's chances of both doing good by improving local economic conditions, and doing well by achieving its organizational goals.

Drawing on the conceptual framework developed in Chapter 1, local actors should choose a theoretical perspective *strategically* consistent with their organizations' aims and capabilities as discussed in Chapter 2. Proper theory increases the chances for effective action. However, local actors must realize that the selection of a particular theory from which to understand economic development, regardless of its explanatory power or degree of realism, essentially determines everything else—the implicit definition of economic development, the aims and purposes of local economic development, preferred economic development strategies, relevant roles of local agencies, and the most appropriate activities to promote local economic development. Why is this so?

The answer may be illustrated by discussing the theoretical perspective on local economic development most frequently used in the United States—the economic base theory or export-base model. From this perspective, the local economy is divided into two economic sectors. The export sector includes all economic activities that generate goods and services that are sold to nonlocal persons, governments, or business entities. The residentiary sector includes all other economic activities that produce for the local market. These two sectors are linked in several ways. First, the export sector directly purchases goods and services from the residentiary sector. Second, workers employed in the export sector purchase food, clothing, shelter, and public services from the residentiary sector. As nonlocal demand for the products of the export sector expands or contracts, the levels of output, income, and employment in the export sector fluctuate in response. Local economic growth is determined by the multiplier effects which are transmitted from the export sector throughout the rest of the local economy (see Hoover 1971, Ch. 8; Uathavikul 1966; and Appendix A, which contrasts economic base theory to stages theory and sector theory).

From this theoretical perspective, the definition of local economic development is assumed to be equivalent to the rate of local economic growth, measured in terms of changes in the local levels of output, income, and employment. The external demand for local exports provides the essential dynamic that stimulates local growth. Although little can be done at the local level to directly increase demand, local economic development strategies can be focused on supporting the expansion of the existing economic base (usually through infrastructure development), developing new export activities (export diversification), and strengthening the linkages between the export sector and the residentiary sector (import substitution). Thus the local economic development strategies designed to facilitate local growth, as supported by economic base theory, usually involve industrial recruitment and promotion and can also include the expansion of existing industries and related improvements in local public infrastructure and services. Thus economic base theory not only provides a specific explanation of economic development; it also suggests a particular definition of economic development and offers support for certain strategies designed to influence the development process. Furthermore, the implicit definition, strategies, and roles for local development organizations are not neutral with respect to the people receiving the benefits or paying the costs of local economic growth. Such is the case with every theory of economic development. In this sense, none is politically neutral. (See Exercise 3.)

Many alternative theories of economic development offer equal or superior explanations of the economic development process compared to economic base theory. Some theories focus on one region, and others examine the more complex interregional context. Some emphasize the initiation of economic development; others stress the diffusion process. Besides economic base theory, the most well-known theories include various theories of regional growth, interregional trade theory which underscores the concepts of absolute and comparative advantage, growth pole theory and the related concepts of growth centers and the urban hierarchy, location theory including central place theory, imperialism and dependency theory, product cycle theory, and spatial theories of entrepreneurship. The suggested theory references include some of the best readings on subnational economic development.

The theories of economic development reviewed below present insights about economic development in qualitative, historical, and dynamic terms. They focus attention on innovation, new company formation, and entrepreneurship. They are most germane to the type of local economic development practice emerging in the United States, which places emphasis on business development and co-development projects. Definitions and strategies are addressed subsequent to the presentation of these theories.

THEORIES

Economic development theory based on interindustry or input-output models usefully extends economic base theory. First, more complexity is taken into account. The interindustry model expresses the linkages between local industries as well as the connections between industries and households, government, and the rest of the world (ROW). Rather than derive a single economic base multiplier through which the stimulus of external demand from the ROW is transmitted, multipliers can be calculated for each industry (see Appendix A). Thus no exclusive classification of industries into export-base or residentiary categories is required. The model shows a much more refined picture of the local growth transmission process.

Second, any sector or grouping of sectors can be treated exogenously. These "final demand" sectors impact upon local output and employment through interindustry linkages. Therefore, external demand for local exports need not be treated as the only source of local growth. The growth stimulus can come from internal or external sources. It may be due to households demanding consumer goods, businesses buying producer goods, or governments procuring various goods and services.

Third, the interindustry model can be used to examine qualitative changes occurring over time. Rather than treating the model as an extension of economic base theory, the interindustry perspective can be applied to the analysis of long-term trends. The model can be used to examine the structure of and linkages among local industries as they evolve over time. Changes in industrial mix may be related to changes in the level of local income, employment, or other economic factors. With this application, the interindustry model provides a test of sector theory by showing how the functional specialization of the local economy is evolving. Is the functional specialization changing from primary sectors to secondary sectors and then to tertiary sectors? Is some other developmental path evident?

In summary, interindustry models can be used to gauge the short-term impacts of economic change or the long-term changes in the structure of the local economy. In the former application, the models offer a means of extending economic base theory by analyzing multiplier effects in much greater detail. In the latter case, the models describe the evolution of industrial structure as an articulation of sector theory.

Wilbur Thompson (1968) distinguishes a long-term view from a short-term view in his seminal article on urban economic development. He argues that economic base theory is useful in addressing the short-term issues related to economic growth. In the long-term, however, a locality's stocks of wealth have the largest potential influence on economic development. Local assets include public infrastructure and facilities, the quality of business services, housing, and formal education, research and development capability, the skills of the local work force, and the entrepreneurial and managerial talent locally available.

The quality of local social overhead capital not only influences the area's comparative advantage but more importantly promotes local innovation and experimentation and supports the subsequent standardization of new products. New products tend to have high income elasticity of demand (that is, demand for the product increases faster than income increases) which results in growth rates that are higher than average. Innovation tends to broaden and diversify the export base as a result.

Market power can have a positive impact on local economic development. If dominant local firms are part of national oligopolistic industries, these firms may realize profit margins that are higher than average. These high margins create the potential for higher real wages. If local workers have union representation and bargaining power, they can increase wage levels in these industries. High wages among organized workers tend to pull up wage levels in other sectors (the wage roll-out effect). High wages translate into high incomes which in turn promote more sophisticated local tastes. Local affluence expands the local market for the development of income-elastic new products.

Local economic development is promoted over time due to the mutual dependence and support among the oligopoly sector, new businesses that provide new products or high-quality business and professional services, well-paid workers that are part of high-income households, and high-quality public facilities, services, and infrastructure. Of course, this positive feedback cycle can be reversed if oligopoly sectors become less productive or more competitive or if local innovation declines.

Product cycle theory focuses attention on the innovation process per se. The theory assumes a more-developed region and less-developed region distinguished by their production structure, technology, factor costs, and tastes. Although both regions have access to modern science and technology, new products tend to originate in the developed region because entrepreneurs there innovate to exploit potential local markets for more sophisticated products. Incentives for new consumer products are provided by high relative incomes. New capital goods are prompted by relatively high wages.

The young product initially satisfies local demand in the developed region. As the product matures, it is exported to the less-developed region. When the product is finally standardized, it can be produced in less-developed areas, and a new plant is established there to protect markets created earlier by exports. Interregional development patterns change over time as recurring cycles of new product, maturing product, and standardized product continue.

Product cycle theory underscores the importance of innovation and indicates the links between innovation, industry mix, and economic development. It focuses on the positive feedback generated by the creation and diffusion of productive investments from developed to less-developed areas. In effect, development originates in the more-developed region and is exported to less-developed areas through investment. Less-developed regions experience more rapid economic growth but at a rhythm set in more-developed areas. Growth increases as the rate of diffusion accelerates and as entrepreneurship in less-developed areas improves (see Vernon 1966, Malizia and Reid 1976).

The interest in entrepreneurship as an explanation of economic development has increased sharply recently in reaction to the declining competitive position of U.S. producers in the international economy. Many different theories of entrepreneurship exist, but some are more relevant than others. The theories of Schumpeter, Jacobs, and Shapero are most pertinent.

Joseph Schumpeter (1962) took issue with the static/comparative static conceptions of the economy. He had little patience with equilibrium models based on the assumption of perfect competition. To Schumpeter, economic behavior had to be studied in dynamic, historical terms, in other words as a development process. In his abstract model, one cycle of exchange represents the production and consumption of existing commodities, including the replacement of capital stock and the provision of working capital for established business purposes. The other cycle represents the introduction of "new combinations" which create new products, new markets, new technologies, new resources or inputs, and new organizational forms. (These categories are used to frame the discussion of project identification that is presented in Chapter 5.) In the real world, these cycles interact to create secular change and business cycles. In Schumpeter's terms, innovation forces change through "waves of creative destruction."

While innovation continually disrupts the economic status quo, new combinations become established and are absorbed into the cycle of normal business activity. In the process, certain producers gain market share and monopolistic advantages and form temporarily stable oligopolistic industries. Contrary to the conventional thinking, Schumpeter argues that oligopolists may well offer the highest quality or lowest priced commodities for consumers.

Competition in established markets is not the essential dynamic that drives the system. Rather it is innovation, both as threat and reality, that destroys old forms of economic activity and creates new combinations of activity. Monopolistic advantages are in continual jeopardy as a result.

When a person carries out new combinations, he or she is an entrepreneur. When the innovation takes hold, the person usually attempts to increase and sustain the financial gains of the innovation. At this point entrepreneurship ends, and more typical management and planning activities become dominant. Thus, planners (as defined in Chapter 1) sometimes act as entrepreneurs, but most of the time they are trying to expand or sustain initial advantages.

Schumpeter recognizes that innovation depends upon finance to nurture and support the introduction of new combinations. While most loanable funds are absorbed to maintain physical and working capital devoted to established lines of production, some funds are needed by entrepreneurs. Certainly, entrepreneurs tap their personal savings, the retained earnings of their established businesses, or other forms of personal wealth. However, significant innovations usually require several rounds of financing beyond the initial seed capital. Investment bankers, venture capitalists, and other sources of risk capital provide the needed equity and debt capital infusions. By mobilizing financial resources to support entrepreneurship, these risk capital sources play a vital role in the innovation process. Thus, in presenting a concept of entrepreneurship, Schumpeter also clarifies a financing role that directs money capital from relatively safe and established spheres of investment to riskier yet more profitable new projects.

Schumpeter views economic development as the successful introduction of new combinations. Although he focuses on the *temporal* distribution of economic activity, his ideas are compatible with the spatial development theories of Thompson and the product cycle.

Jane Jacobs relates the economic viability of cities to the creation of new work by entrepreneurs. Complementing Schumpeter, she argues against an efficiency orientation which may yield profitability and growth but seldom sustained economic development. The creation of new work is a messy process that is fraught with trials, experimentation, failures, and redundancies. Her vivid contrast of Manchester, the city efficient, to Birmingham, the city of small enterprises, assigns long-term advantage to places with people who can keep adapting to environmental change by creating opportunities for new work (see Jacobs 1969, especially pp. 86–96).

Albert Shapero uses Jacobs's contrast to characterize this adaptability as resilience, the quality related to creativity, initiative, and diversity that leads to self-sustaining and self-renewing local economies. Entrepreneurs are the people who act creatively and boldly. They innovate by forming new companies which are the vehicles of innovation. Thus, entrepreneurship represents the essential dynamic of local development (see Shapero 1981 and Appendix B).

DEFINITIONS

Economic development may be defined in many different ways, depending upon one's explicit or implicit theoretical perspective. Some definitions focus on the *results* of economic development. These results affect each individual or the community representing the population of individuals. These impacts are both economic and social or social-psychological. Instead of results, other definitions emphasize the characteristics of the local economy itself, as shown in Table 2.

The definition of local economic development should be carefully considered at the conceptual level. Each theory of economic development offers a foundation from which a definition can be drawn. Economic base theory, for example, would have you define local economic development as the rate of growth in output, income, or employment generated locally, and the creation of more work in and because of the export sector. Interindustry models would shift attention to the temporal changes in industry mix as well as overall local economic growth. At the community level, Thompson's growth model emphasizes the quality of local stocks of wealth—public and private, human and material. At the individual level, increases in personal income and improved occupational mix reflect improvements in local economic development. Product cycle theory views economic development as a process of initiation and diffusion of new products. In some localities, economic development is reflected in new product innovation, but in other places it depends on the introduction of standardized products. In the former places local economic development is defined in terms of the qualitative changes

TABLE 2. Possible Definitions of Economic Development

	Definitions	
	Individual level	Community level
Results of economic development		
Social psychological impacts	Improves human well-being	Improves the community quality of life
Economic impacts	Increases consumption and material welfare	Improves the distribution of wealth or opportunities
Theories of economic development		
Economic base theory	More work	Economic growth
Interindustry models	Different work	Evolving industrial mix
Thompson's growth model	Better work	Improving social overhead capital and other stocks of wealth
Product cycle theory	Initiation and diffusion of new products	
Entrepreneurship theories		
Schumpeter	Innovation	New combinations
Jacobs	New work	Dynamism and adaptability
Shapero	Creativity and initiative	Resilience and diversity

Source: Compiled by author.

resulting from better work, higher personal incomes, product innovation, and possibly industrial diversification. In contrast, economic development in localities dominated by standardized products is equivalent to economic growth. The rate of economic growth depends directly on the attraction of companies producing standardized products and indirectly on the ability to keep local wage and income levels relatively low.

Theories stressing the importance of entrepreneurship suggest definitions in terms of the innovativeness and the resulting dynamism of the local economy. Schumpeter argues that individual entrepreneurs introduce new combinations, and, in the aggregate, entrepreneurship provides the essential dynamic of the economic development process because it creates new markets, products, and industries. Similarly, Jacobs defines economic development in terms of people creating new work that results in adaptive and dynamic cities. Shapero sees economic development as creativity among initiative-taking individuals that leads to resilience and diversity at the community level.

These definitions harken back to the planning framework discussed in Chapter 1 in that they focus on different aspects of the purposive activity of work. The definitions illustrate different ways that work can be planned relative to existing forms of work: economic development is the generation of more work; economic development is the provision of better work; economic development is the creation of opportunities to carry out new work. Each definition may be related to a different set of organizational goals and objectives. To some extent, each suggests different economic development strategies.

The precise definition selected will contain strong implications for the recommended strategies, tactics, and roles which are consistent with it. For example, Malizia and Rubin (1983) advance a discussion of local economic development that demonstrates the connections between a particular definition of economic development, the related economic development strategies and tools, the ways to structure local development organizations, and compatible roles for local professionals. (See Exercise 4.)

In practice, few people will have the authority to pursue their unique definition of local economic development on behalf of the entire community. Most will be under strong pressure to accept the view of local economic development held by officials, business leaders, or other locally influential people. In the overwhelming number of U.S. communities, economic development is defined primarily as job creation (the generation of more work) with some regard for the stability of the existing employment base and secondarily as tax-base enhancement with the related interest in the real estate development or redevelopment potentials of commercial and industrial areas.

In summary, the most popular understanding of economic development (economic base theory) and the most common definition of local economic development (job creation and retention) do not do justice to the richness or complexity of the subject. Yet in deference to the realities faced by local actors, we shall accept this definition and move on to consider the most relevant strategies and tactics. Definitional issues will crop up again, however, in Chapter 4 where we consider criteria for financing local business development and in Chapter 5 where we consider criteria for project evaluation. (See Exercise 5.)

STRATEGIES

Which strategies should local actors consider if job creation and retention are the basic community goals of economic development and these goals are compatible with their organization's aims? The question may be best answered by raising several questions. First, making use of the organizational planning framework, which investment decisions affect most directly the creation or retention of jobs? In the U.S. economy, the planners in the private sector provide over 80 percent of all jobs. This source of jobs is more important than either the public sector or the nonprofit sector. Moreover, investment decisions that provide permanent and stable employment opportunities are far more important than investment decisions that result in temporary jobs, highly unstable jobs, or no jobs at all. Notwithstanding the importance of the construction industry and the housing sector to the national economy, we are reasonable not to focus on residential development as the backbone of a jobs-oriented strategy due to the temporary nature of much of this employment.[1] Furthermore, it is reasonable to ignore seasonal or migrant employment, rapidly declining industries, and the self-employed in designing job-oriented strategies.

Second, which business investment decisions impact most positively on job creation and retention? This question has been the subject of much ongoing debate. Recent research has underscored the importance of small business development in the job creation process, but many issues remain unresolved. For example, whether the small-business sector is as autonomous or dynamic as many suggest, or whether it is dependent on big business is not clear. Also, we are not sure whether, relative to job creation potential, size is a more essential attribute of the firm than its age, organizational status, industry, or management. Whatever the causal factors, the research does reveal that business development in the United States is a very volatile process. Job growth and decline results from the births, deaths, expansions, and contractions among a minority of establishments and firms. The majority of business entities maintain a relatively stable employment base over time.[2]

On the other hand, we may safely say that most merger and acquisition activities of big business are irrelevant with respect to new employment in that these activities change claims on existing business assets without creating new capacity. To the extent that mergers and acquisitions result in the dissipation of corporate earnings and available credit, these activities may have the effect of eliminating more employment than they create.

Using the research reported in Armington and Odle (1982), we may identify two groups of firms for considering strategies. Small firms having fewer than 100 employees tend to be single establishment firms, independent, younger, and more labor-intensive, and are among all sectors of the economy, but especially in agriculture, construction, and trade. Large firms with 100 employees or more are often multilocational or multiestablishment entities with more capital-intensive facilities. Large firms are the more mature and dominate the mining, manufacturing, and transportation/communications/ public utilities sectors. In general, small firms are locally based concerns serving local, regional, or national markets, while large firms are typically oriented to national or international markets and are usually headquartered outside of the area.

Local actors interested in job creation and retention must consider a full range of strategies to support both small firms and large firms—what we will call *business development strategies*. These strategies are defined as a reflection of the dynamics of the firm. In other words, firm births, deaths, expansions, contractions, and stability may be encouraged, sustained, or discouraged through the application of certain local strategies. Firm dynamics and the related development strategies are listed in Table 3.

The nine strategies may be described briefly, as follows:

● Industrial recruitment/promotion—advertise, provide information, develop infrastructure and sites, and offer financial and tax incentives to attract new establishments of national concerns into an area.

● Expansion of existing industries—provide infrastructure, financing, skills training, and marketing assistance to support the expansion of larger manufacturers already in an area.

TABLE 3. Firm Dynamics and Business Development Strategies for Job Creation/Retention

From the perspective of the local economy

Large, nonlocal firms may plan to	Business development strategy
Establish a new branch plant (birth)	→ Industrial recruitment/promotion
Expand an existing local branch	→ Expansion of existing industries
Close a branch or subsidiary (death)	→ Worker/community ownership
Contract a local facility	→ Technical assistance
Maintain a stable employment level	→ Management assistance

Small, local firms plan to	
Start up (birth)	→ New enterprise development
Expand	→ Small business development
Close (death)	→ Transition to new ownership
Contract	→ Technical assistance
Remain stable	→ Management assistance

Large or small firms may plan to	
Acquire or sell an existing local concern	→ Brokerage/financing services

Source: Compiled by author.

● Worker/community ownership—help organize new ownership groups, help negotiate terms of purchase, and provide financing and other support to transfer ownership to area residents.

● New enterprise development—help identify feasible ventures, the people to initiate them, and the initial sources of financing.

● Small business development—offer business counseling, business planning and financing to expand local retail, service, and smaller manufacturing enterprises.

● Transition to new ownership—a long-term strategy of finding viable privately held businesses that do not have heirs, matching them with potential new owners, and structuring the acquisition financing needed to sustain the businesses as going concerns and to secure adequate compensation for the original owners.

• Brokerage/financing services—assist in sales and acquisitions by identifying and matching owners seeking to sell concerns with potential buyers, and secure financing from local investors and financial intermediaries in order to maintain employment levels in these businesses.

• Technical assistance—define and solve specific technical, production or marketing problems to arrest the contraction of local concerns; and

• Management assistance—provide general advice and assistance to enhance the viability of stable local concerns.

Note that the elements of these strategies are not mutually exclusive but overlap considerably. What makes each strategy unique is the purpose to which each set of strategic elements is directed, namely to births, deaths, expansions, contractions, stabilization, or transfer of business entities. The elements of these strategies are discussed in greater detail in the next section.

Local strategies need not be designed for each dynamic case because the appropriate strategic mix will be a function of specific economic conditions and the size of the locality. Yet we must describe the nine unique strategies here so that local actors have the benefit of considering as many relevant business development options as possible. The range of local development strategies usually discussed is clearly far narrower than the potential range suggested by the dynamics of U.S. firms. Since local economic development practice is dominated by the strategy of industrial recruitment and promotion, very few other business development strategies have received adequate attention.

Criteria are needed to evaluate and compare the nine strategies. Let us adapt the framework used by investment portfolio managers for this purpose. Like portfolio managers, local actors are trying to find optimal investment strategies that put limited developmental resources to their best use. Like portfolio managers, they must weigh alternatives in the face of an uncertain future. Just as private investments are compared on the basis of risk and reward, the criteria of social risk and expected social reward can be used to assess local strategic alternatives.

The private risk–reward criteria must be modified in one significant way. Unlike portfolio managers whose major objective is the creation and retention of *wealth* over time, local actors are primarily

FIG. 4. Risk–Reward Framework

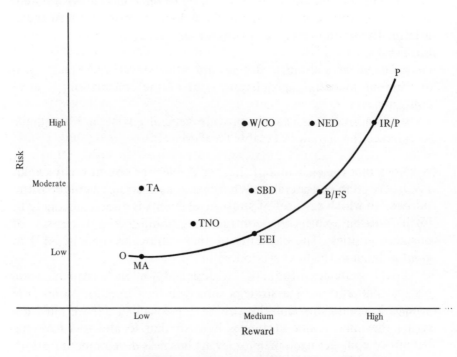

BUSINESS DEVELOPMENT STRATEGIES

OP   —Optimum portfolio of strategies
W/CO—Worker/community ownership
NED —New enterprise development
IR/P —Industrial recruitment/promotion
TA   —Technical assistance
SBD —Small business development
B/FS —Brokerage/financing services
TNO —Transition to new ownership
EEI   —Expansion of existing industries
MA   —Management assistance

interested in the creation and retention of permanent *jobs*. In reference to Table 3, business planners usually apply a risk–reward analysis when making the investment decisions realized in the actions listed in the left-hand column. Those responsible for local economic development are advised to analyze the strategies listed in the right-hand column from a similar risk–reward perspective.[3]

The nine business development strategies are arrayed in Figure 4 applying the risk–reward framework to a "typical" community. Obviously, the array will change for different communities. Reward, of course, is measured not as dollar return on investment but as the number of jobs created or retained per dollar expended. Strategies that yield the greatest amount of person-years of work over the long term generate the greatest rewards.[4] Risk is reckoned as the probability that the strategy will fail to create or retain the expected jobs. To compare the strategies, think of each point (strategy) as representing a long-term, alternative deployment of the same total amount of real resources.

If the risk–reward estimates given in Figure 4 were correct, local actors could use this mapping to select an "optimum portfolio" of business development strategies, represented in Figure 4 by the line segment OP. The optimum strategic portfolio is a conceptualization that underscores the importance of considering a full *range* of strategies. Attention to risk–reward criteria warns against selecting any single strategy regardless of its attractiveness on a priori grounds. Neither should consideration be restricted to the nine strategies presented above. Consider as many potential strategies as possible (using brainstorming techniques if they are helpful). Avoid the temptation to mimic another locality, follow the prescription of a single national policy, or listen to only one local interest group. Try not to put all your eggs in one basket.

The most popular economic development strategies are industrial recruitment and promotion and downtown revitalization. Industrial recruitment and promotion will receive no further treatment in this book because the approach is quite well known. The American Economic Development Council accredits Basic Economic Development Courses throughout the country which teach recruitment and promotion skills. Industrial developers are well versed in these skills and can assist communities wanting to pursue this strategy. Downtown revitalization has received similar emphasis. Although real estate development is not considered separately as a business development strategy, we will consider real estate projects along with business development projects in Chapters 6, 7, and 8. On the other hand, far less formal consideration has been given to business development strategies which could complement industrial recruitment and downtown revitalization, and thereby diversify the approach to local economic development. In many localities, these strategies offer the best approaches to job creation and retention.

Five of the remaining eight strategies are discussed in the next section. Management assistance to assist stable businesses and technical assistance to arrest business contractions are not treated separately because the elements of these strategies are covered in the discussions of other strategies. Transition to new ownership to prevent the closure of a small firm essentially combines the features of worker/community ownership and brokerage/financing services. Its major unique aspect is matching new owners with existing owners several years before the closure is contemplated.

TOOLS AND TACTICS

Elements of the following business development strategies are discussed in this section: expansion of existing industries, small business development, new enterprise development, worker or community ownership, and brokerage and financing services. These strategies share some important assumptions and features. All five strategies attempt to build on resources that already exist in the local economy: natural resources, existing businesses, and, most importantly, the talents, skills, and energies of the local population. They are realized through business development projects initiated to strengthen the local commercial and industrial sectors. They are guided by people living in the area, sometimes with assistance from the state or federal government or other outside sources. LDO executives are assumed to provide leadership in formulating and implementing appropriate strategies.

Although strategies that build on local resources and talents have relevance to all communities, they are absolutely essential for revitalizing economically depressed areas and locations that have little potential or are unattractive to new branch plants recruited to a state.

Expansion of Existing Industries

In communities that have a manufacturing base, opportunities often exist for assisting individual companies to expand. The companies under discussion here are distinguished from small trade, service, and distribution firms (discussed below under Small Business Development, next) in two major ways. First, they have greater need for physical capital: land, infrastructure (roads, water lines, rail spurs, etc.), buildings, and equipment. Second, they are likely to be more stable enterprises, with greater financial solvency and more solid management. These stable enterprises often have trouble finding new avenues of expansion and ways to finance growth.

Programs for expanding industries generally offer two types of assistance: infrastructure development and financing for plant and equipment purchases. Additional types of assistance, presently under-utilized, are skills training for a company that is increasing its work force and marketing through product matching and export promotion.

Helping local industries expand can be quite worthwhile in areas that have a manufacturing base and a relatively healthy economy. The approach builds on existing investment in the community; it is a moderate risk, since it targets existing companies of some proven permanence; it can result in the creation of relatively large numbers of jobs; and it bolsters *local* companies that already have some commitment to the area. Expansions can have significant multiplier effects in the local economy when the expanding firm has links with local suppliers and distributors (recall economic base theory and input–output analysis).

The LDO executive can help to provide infrastructure for industry, particularly in cities where basic facilities like water and sewer services are lacking. Industrial parks are particularly appropriate in rural areas because they are economical and save land for agriculture, forestry, and other nonindustrial uses by concentrating industrial activity in a small area.

Developing industrial infrastructure makes most sense when it is designed to meet the needs of locally owned plants that have already made a commitment to expand in the area. Many cities that constructed industrial parks, usually with federal aid, learned a costly lesson when they unsuccessfully tried to recruit tenants after building the park. Today they own idle, expensive infrastructure.

Many businesses have trouble obtaining long-term loans for the purchase of land, buildings, and equipment. The public sector has tried to provide long-term, fixed-asset financing for growth through, for example, industrial revenue bonds, state industrial development authorities, local development corporations, and various federal programs. Another vehicle for responding to capital needs of expanding businesses is the revolving loan fund (mentioned below under Small Business Development and discussed more fully in the next chapter).

Skills training is most often used as a means of meeting the work force needs of expanding businesses. In some instances, the absence of an appropriately trained work force has caused plants to seek new locations for expansion. A publicly funded training program may allow a company to expand locally. Another role for subsidized training is helping to ensure that a number of economically disadvantaged people are hired when local industries expand.

Product matching and export promotion involve helping local firms expand their markets. Product matching systems range from computerized listings of buyers and sellers classified by seven-digit commodity codes to engineering services that assist buyers in new product design and in finding the vendors capable of manufacturing the new product.

Export promotion activities may involve helping local industries make use of the state or federal programs designed to achieve this end (for example, programs of the U.S. Department of Commerce, the Small Business Administration, and the Export-Import Bank). Activities may also involve setting up area export development councils or a foreign trade zone, seeking the assistance of export management firms, or even organizing an export trading company.

In summary, the industrial expansion strategy can be an effective approach to local economic development when there is a diverse local economy, a solid base of locally owned industries, and local support for industrial development. When these conditions obtain, assistance with infrastructure development and financing can make the expansion of local industries more affordable. The training component provides a ready work force and helps ensure that local people, including economically disadvantaged persons, benefit from expansion efforts. Marketing assistance is a more sophisticated activity to involve local development organizations more directly in the expansion of existing industries. Market studies that can support these emerging techniques are discussed in Chapter 8.

Small Business Development

In most communities, small businesses (firms with less than 100 employees) are the mainstay of the local economy. These firms dominate the trade, service, and distribution sectors but are represented in all sectors. Most are owner operated. Many represent small capital investments and generate low rates of profit. Owners often have little or no formal business training. In management capability, the businesses range from ones in which the owner may lack even basic skills in bookkeeping, financial planning, and marketing, to businesses run by capable entrepreneurs who are beset by more complex growth problems, such as personnel management and tax planning, and consequently need more sophisticated business skills. Most small businesses raise debt capital from commercial banks. But for several reasons, they have considerable difficulty borrowing capital at affordable rates: they may lack sufficient collateral, they may not present a convincing business prospectus, or they may be perceived by lenders and investors as very high-risk ventures.

An effective small business development strategy must address the basic needs of small businesses for financial, managerial, and technical assistance. It aims to help new businesses expand into more profitable and viable concerns. As these needs are met, new jobs are created, incomes of owners and workers increase, and an important component of the local employment equation becomes more stable.

Business counseling is the least expensive and possibly the most cost-effective approach to small-business development, particularly in areas where many small-business owners are untrained in financial analysis, marketing, and business planning. Efforts to assist them need not always be sophisticated or complex to be of real help. A local development organization staffed by a generalist who has access to consultants for specialized technical or managerial problems can be quite effective in helping businesses improve their profitability, assess their potential for expansion, and even obtain bank financing. Hiring a person with business experience who can communicate well with local business owners seems more appropriate than hiring one who has formal business training.

The essence of counseling and technical assistance lies in helping the business owner identify and solve his or her specific problems. The business plan often utilized is one which leads the business owner through a series of questions about goals, the current state of business, known risks, and other basic issues (see Bangs and Osgood 1978). More sophisticated expertise is needed for these forms of technical assistance.

Although business counseling programs can help small businesses obtain bank financing, a need to supplement commercially available assistance often exists. State and local programs offer supplementary financing to small businesses using several vehicles, the most prevalent of which are direct loans, loan guarantees, and equity investments.

Direct loans serve several interrelated functions: they can make capital available to businesses that could not otherwise get a loan; they can increase the amount of money a business can borrow by leveraging bank financing; and they can lower the cost of capital by offering below-market interest rates.

The most effective kind of small business development program is one that combines business counseling with financing services. In the coming years, however, establishing revolving loan funds will be a more difficult matter since few sources of financing remain viable.[5] LDO directors may be able to argue effectively for the capitalization of revolving loan funds by state governments or local sources since a one-time commitment of funds can be recycled through the local economy for years to come. (See Chapter 4.)

The success of business counseling and revolving loan programs indicates that, in many communities, a supportive climate can draw out viable business proposals and help business firms expand (or stabilize). In other localities, this strategy may not be adequate to reverse negative economic trends and a pervasive atmosphere of pessimism. In these instances, LDO staff should go beyond management assistance, technical assistance, and financing, and take more active roles as initiators of new enterprises.

New Enterprise Development

The less economic activity an area has, the smaller the economic foundation on which to build, but the greater the role for the LDO director interested in initiating new enterprises. The new enterprise development approach requires research on local opportunities for new businesses and active solicitation of people to start such businesses. In some cases, the ventures could be started by the LDO itself. The strategy requires a strong LDO leadership capable of providing effective management and technical assistance. The strategy is rather risky, but it can also have a greater impact on local employment. At its best, this strategy can lead to the creation of a network of local businesses that build on local resources and create local linkages.

When seeking opportunities for new enterprise development, the LDO staff should begin by conducting an inventory of the local economy. The first thing to look for is underutilized resources: natural resources, human resources, or infrastructure that could provide the bases for new businesses.

Natural resource-based development is of particular interest in rural areas with renewable resources that have never been tapped to their full potential. Natural resource-based development not only creates new jobs by spawning new ventures, it also enables people who are already making a marginal living through farming, fishing, logging, and similar occupations to raise their incomes and gain a more stable livelihood. Development based on natural resources may utilize waste products, build on skills already present in the local population, and generate labor-intensive activities.

The inventory of the local economy should consider the input requirements of local businesses, especially manufacturers. Local businesses may be importing items that could be produced locally. Investigation of new product ideas for local manufacturers may also be appropriate. These efforts could be tied into a product matching system or export promotion mechanism, both of which were discussed above.

After a product or service has been identified, developed, and test-marketed, the LDO director would either find a capable manager to operate the business or found the enterprise as a LDO subsidiary. To initiate the venture, both debt and equity financing must be arranged and properly structured.

Worker/Community Ownership

Plant closings have become a familiar feature of many local economies. Even localities in high-growth regions experience significant job loss due to plant closings. International competition, federal tax laws, and other factors will inspire business planners to increase capital mobility and asset redeployment. Thus, local strategies appropriate to the reality of increasingly frequent plant closing are clearly needed.

Many economists and financial analysts argue against all efforts to avoid plant closings. Their arguments have force under one condition: when plant, equipment, and inventory are obsolete, making it impossible for the concern to become competitive. In other instances, worker or community ownership to prevent a plant closing offers substantial rewards although it remains a high-risk strategy.

Ideally LDO directors require sufficient time to complete a market feasibility study, the result of either an effective early warning system or timely information from the firm's management. The study should examine the pros and cons of continuing operations and the probability of and time needed for turning a profit.

LDO staff should help organize new ownership groups and access the legal and technical assistance needed to establish a new ownership entity. Assistance is available in many parts of the country. Capable organizations offer training and technical assistance to local groups interested in this strategy (see Redburn and Buss 1982).

LDO directors should not negotiate terms of purchase on anyone's behalf; rather they should serve as facilitators who encourage a successful process. They should also help mobilize the debt and equity financing needed to consummate the project and provide other support as required.

Proper timing and accurate information are very important. The record on worker and community buy-outs shows that these groups often purchase assets too late and pay too much for them. Part of the problem stems from incomplete and tardy information provided by the selling concern and from the lack of experience of the buyers. However, another aspect of the problem stems from the difference between going-concern value and liquidation or forced-sale value.

A viable business may be valued as a going concern by capitalizing its expected future income stream at some normal rate of profit or expected rate of return on investment. That same business in a dormant state and being sold off (liquidated) asset by asset has a forced-sale value that is much lower than its going-concern value. Many worker and community groups do not understand this distinction. The buy-out comes too late to purchase a profitable going concern but too early to take advantage of bargain prices of assets sold at auction. LDO staff should help ascertain a fair value for the facility. Business valuation is explored in Chapter 7.

Another issue relates to the variation in expected rates of profit and return. Generally, large multiestablishment businesses expect higher returns than smaller independent businesses. Often, the difference is substantial. For example, conglomerates may sell off any facilities not yielding more than 20 percent return on investment while independent firms operating these facilities would find 10 percent quite acceptable. No absolute standard indicates economic viability in an uncertain and changing world. Assuming that workers and community groups will be satisfied with lower returns in order to retain local jobs, local leaders should look closely at the status of all major facilities owned by national concerns to gauge their attractiveness as candidates for this strategy.

Most national concerns place a large burden on local facilities in the form of general administrative and overhead charges. They usually repatriate the profits to headquarters. The possibility of mismanagement due to absentee control should also be mentioned. These factors tend to make local facilities more viable under local ownership.

On the other hand, the risks of worker or community ownership should not be overlooked. Mobilizing a competent management team and developing good working relationships among production workers, managers, and top planners are difficult tasks. LDO directors should try to offer advice and technical assistance but should not assume any responsibility for the ultimate success or failure of the worker/community-owned firm.

Brokerage/Financing Services

Unlike residential real estate, most businesses are sold by owners without the help of brokers. Moreover, the majority of businesses are sold without any real estate (land or buildings) being transacted.

Local development organizations may assist in the sale and purchase of existing local concerns. The LDO director interested in brokerage as a job retention strategy must gain the confidence of the business community by stressing the discretion and confidentiality

TABLE 4. Tactical Elements of Business Development Strategies

Element	Industrial recruitment/promotion	Expansion of existing industries	Worker/community ownership	New enterprise development	Small business development	Transition to new ownership	Brokerage/financial services
Advertising locality or businesses to local or national prospects	a						a
Identification of worker/ community group, would-be entrepreneur, or buyer			a	a		a	
Identification of viable new venture, viable existing business, or seller				a		a	a
Matching of buyers/sellers				b		b	a
Negotiating sales/purchases			b			b	
Business counseling or other management assistance				a	b		
Business planning, financial analysis, or other technical assistance		b	a		a		
Marketing assistance		a	b	a	a	b	
Skills training	b	b		b			
Tax incentives	b						
Industrial site development	a						
Infrastructure development	a	a					
Financing assistance	a	a	a	a	a	a	a

a = major element;
b = minor element.

Source: Compiled by author.

of the services. Obviously, public agencies could not give assurances of confidentiality.

Brokerage services aim at quantity, seeking as many potential sellers and interested buyers as possible. The services match potential sellers and buyers. They may be quite impersonal, involving coded listings that are distributed or sold to principals requesting the information, or more personal and intensive in terms of matching particular buyers and sellers and negotiating mutually acceptable terms. For intensive brokerage services, the LDO should charge a fee.

Many sales can be consummated without external financing. The combination of seller financing and buyer equity is sufficient, particularly for smaller concerns. In other cases, external financing is required. Financial assistance services range from simply introducing buyers to loan officers, investors, or administrators of public financing sources, to more active involvement in assisting buyers that want to access funds from external sources.

By way of summary, the business development strategies and the tactical elements of each are shown in Table 4 (see also Bergman 1981, Malizia and Rubin 1982 and 1983, Regional Planning Commission 1981, and U.S. Conference of Mayors 1980). Notice that financing is a central requirement to all of these business development strategies. Because of its special importance, Chapter 4 explores ways to capitalize and manage a local business development fund. (See Exercise 6.)

LOCAL DEVELOPMENT ORGANIZATIONS

As noted, local actors can initiate and implement these business development strategies or broader economic development strategies most effectively through LDOs. Since economic development is a long, protracted process, strong committed leadership is needed to sustain the effort. This leadership can be exercised more effectively if it operates through and is supported by a LDO.

Most local economic development opportunities are not profitable enough to interest a strictly for-profit organization. On the other hand, the amount of flexibility and entrepreneurship required to execute many economic development strategies is too much to expect from most public agencies. The LDO assumes a middle ground, being concerned with the well-being of the entire community yet operating strategically and tactically like a well-run business. It might take the legal form of a private nonprofit association, federation, co-operative, or multipurpose corporation.

Successful LDOs of whatever form share certain characteristics. The characteristics most important to success are: flexibility, strong and creative leadership, solid local support, adequate funding, and competent, dedicated staff. These characteristics are discussed below.

Flexibility includes a willingness to experiment and an ability to learn from mistakes, to respond to changing circumstances, and to seize opportunities when they arise. Some LDOs have evolved from conducting one-shot demonstration projects to administering a longer-term, special purpose program, finally becoming an ongoing, general purpose organization. LDO directors must continually reassess project activities and explore new strategies to discover the right mix of marketable activities that provides a stable base of support.

Some LDO directors carry flexibility too far. They take on a wide range of disparate activities based on the availability of funding. An organization with limited staff may spread itself too thin and lose its primary focus on economic or business development strategies.

Effective LDO directors have a vision of how the local economy can be developed. For commitment to be sustained over a long period, they must realize that rewards will be slow to come. In many instances, a period of intensive community education is necessary. Usually the LDO must cultivate good relationships with bankers and business leaders and stay aloof from electoral politics.

Since a LDO functions best as catalyst and facilitator, rather than as independent actor, it needs a broad base of local support to be successful. One of the first audiences with whom an LDO director must win credibility is the local business community, and particu-larly the bankers and investors. If the organization is to gain support in that quarter, the director must emphasize the intention to help local businesses and banks, not compete with them. She or he must convince the local financial/business establishment that the operation of a revolving loan fund, for example, will not take business away from local banks, but will instead open up new projects for bank participation and help develop new businesses. The political support of other local groups should be pursued after gaining acceptance by the local business community.

Closely related to the issue of local support is the question of the amount of territory a LDO should attempt to serve. From the standpoint of maintaining a strong local presence and achieving a visible impact, a smaller geographic area is better. From the standpoint of serving populations large enough to secure political strength and a solid funding base, a larger territory is more sensible.

Although some LDO directors use volunteers, paid staff is needed to operate successfully. As discussed earlier, many successful development organizations believe that it is most important to hire staff who know the local area and who can communicate with local people. Technical skills such as business counselling or loan packaging can be learned on the job or supplied by experienced local people willing to work with the staff; basic interpersonal skills are harder to acquire.

Fund raising is a constant struggle for LDO staff. Most have relied on state and federal grants to help cover administrative costs, staff salaries, and project financing. Federally funded employment and housing programs have provided the start-up money for many LDOs, enabling them to operate their first projects and plan succeeding ones. With cutbacks in and elimination of several of the primary federal funding sources, they are seeking new sources of support. Although not an easy task, fund raising does provide an indicator of the ability to convince local people of the relevance of LDO efforts. Some organizations have obtained funds from foundations, churches, and local governments. Others subsist partly with the aid of small annual membership dues or contributions from local corporations. Another possibility is to receive a modest share of profits from the operations of a business subsidiary if a new enterprise development strategy is pursued. Still another option is to administer the local business development fund and use income from loan servicing to finance staff, following the example of the SBA 503 program (see Chapter 4).

Regardless of the overall funding picture, local fund raising is a good strategy, because it allows the organization to build local support while it is raising money. Obviously it will be difficult to promote local economic development without a solid base of local support, as noted in Chapter 2.

Ideally the LDO can help formulate the best economic and business development strategies, serve as an initiator, catalyst, and facilitator of local co-development projects, and provide a source of technical and financial assistance to local businesses. Some of the most appropriate roles for LDO staff include business counseling, market research, venture initiation, loan packaging, project financing, industrial development, and development facilitation. The particular range of activities that are undertaken should be responsive to local circumstances: the services lacking in the area, the capacity of the local economy to use new services, and the aims, ability, and resources of the organization itself. Few organizations, of course, spring up full-blown, performing the complete array of development functions. Most organizations evolve over a period of years, adding some functions and dropping others on the basis of what works most effectively. (See Malizia and Rubin 1983 for descriptions of exemplary LDOs.)

One way to tackle the problem of LDO role definition is to identify the key local actors and, for any given strategy that the locality wants to pursue, list the different tools available at the local level. The LDO role should be defined in relation to the roles of other key actors. (See Exercise 7.)

NOTES

1. Although not addressed at the strategic level, real estate development to promote commercial and industrial development is included in the project level discussions of Chapters 5 through 8. The Urban Land Institute publishes a good deal of excellent information on public–private partnerships and co-development aspects of local real estate development and redevelopment projects.

2. Recent research done at the Brookings Institution for SBA reports on the dynamics of all U.S. firms and small U.S. firms in the late 1970s. While employment in slightly more than half of all firms did not change, a significant amount of employment change occurred in the rest. Employment increased due to births and expansions of establishments and decreased due to deaths (closures) and contractions. For example, total private employment in the U.S. increased by 8.3 percent from 1978 to 1980. On average, each 1.0 percent increase in employment resulted from a 1.0 percent increase in births, a 0.7 percent decrease from deaths, a 1.7 percent increase from expansions, and a 1.0 percent decrease due to contractions. The figures for small firms were similar in that net expansion of existing establishments was a more important source of employment growth than births less deaths. See Armington and Odle (1982).

3. Michael Conroy (1975) has applied portfolio theory to examine regional economic growth. He views the ideal portfolio as the mix of industries that

optimizes a combination of strength for growth and diversity for stability. Here the portfolio approach is used to consider an optimal mix of strategies for local economic development.

4. Although difficult to predict, the number of jobs created over the life of the businesses generated through local strategies should be estimated. For each business, annual estimates of average full-time employment should be made. Because investments made in capital stock are fully amortized in 18 years, estimates of permanent jobs associated with this capital should be limited to the same time frame.

If annual estimates were the same over time for each business, the sum or average employment figures could be used equivalently. However, if estimates varied over time, the total person-years of work created should be considered. Assuming that a job now is worth more than a job later, the time series of annual employment estimates should be discounted at a positive rate. As a result businesses that create more person-years of work in the early years evidence higher rewards than businesses that offer the same total person-years of work later in the life of the facility. Furthermore, localities with more pressing and immediate job needs should use a higher discount rate than localities taking a longer-term

4

FINANCING LOCAL BUSINESS DEVELOPMENT STRATEGIES

Of the array of tools with which to pursue various economic and business development strategies, financing deserves particular attention. Local actors must consider how to secure funds for development and how to deploy funds to support the execution of any local economic development strategy. Traditionally, localities have sought federal grants to fund economic development planning and economic development projects. Funds were used primarily for public infrastructure development to support commercial or industrial development. Other sources include local tax revenues, state government transfers, and debt capital raised by local borrowing.

Most municipal borrowings have taken the form of general obligation bonds, although revenue bonds have come increasingly popular. General obligation bonds are backed by the full faith, credit, and taxing power of the municipality offering them. Revenue bonds are backed by the income-generating potential of the public investment being financed. Consequently, the former have been used to pay for public facilities such as schools, libraries, and government buildings. The revenue bonds have underwritten the construction of hospitals and health clinics, airports, and utilities. Traditionally, revenue bonds were thought to be more risky than general obligation bonds and carried a higher rate of interest, reflecting the higher-risk premium. However, this differential is disappearing when the financial soundness of a community is less certain than the potential revenues from a particular local investment.[1]

Housing and real estate development investments to meet social objectives have traditionally used public financing to stimulate private participation in community development. Most effort has been devoted to neighborhood improvements, subsidized housing construction, mixed-use developments, downtown revitalization, and industrial development. For industrial development, local jurisdictions have built industrial parks, extended water and sewer lines, improved roads and other infrastructure, and constructed parking facilities, water and waste water treatment facilities, and recreational facilities. In some places, these investments have been successful in providing leverage for additional private investments. In other instances public investments have not returned benefits in terms of job creation and tax base improvements to justify their costs.

Commercial real estate development is usually financed *jointly* from public and private sources. For industrial development, joint financing is initiated through federal loan and loan guarantee programs for new branch plants and other industrial facilities from the Farmers Home Administration (FmHA) or the Small Business Administration (SBA). Most states authorize the use of industrial revenue bonds (IRBs) and business development loan pools to provide debt capital to companies at market or below-market rates. In the area of business development, local public–private ventures are much less common.

The traditional sources of funds for local development have been seriously attacked in recent years. Federal grants, loans, and loan guarantee programs administered by the domestic assistance agencies have been reduced or terminated. The volume of IRBs has been curtailed in an effort to reduce the loss of federal tax revenues. At the same time, financial intermediaries are investing more heavily in national money markets, increasing the outflow of funds from most localities to the largest money centers.

Changes in the federal tax laws in 1981 and 1982 have reduced incentives to high-income individuals to invest in tax-exempt securities while creating new incentives for other forms of private investment. Federal tax incentives designed to increase the *rate* of private investment have also increased its spatial *mobility*, decreasing job security and undermining the long-term effectiveness of traditional economic development strategies. New business development strategies, such as those discussed in Chapter 3, are emerging in response to the greater volatility of the local economy. These strategies are best executed through a local development organization that has access to a local, publicly controlled source of development funds.

To finance business development strategies in the face of these realities, local development organizations must secure alternative sources of financing, develop new financial instruments, and involve more local investors. One alternative is to capitalize a business development fund with emphasis on local sources. Once capitalized, the fund must be well managed. Effectively capitalizing and managing a local business development fund is no small challenge. The key questions are: How can local actors create and effectively manage a local pool of funds to support business development strategies and to finance the assets of specific business development projects? How can the continuation of a viable fund be assured?

CAPITALIZING LOCAL BUSINESS DEVELOPMENT FUNDS

To capitalize the fund initially, viable federal sources of funds and available state sources should be made accessible. Some communities already have experience administering a revolving loan fund. As noted in Chapter 3, several federal agencies have devoted small amounts of resources to provide initial capitalizations. For example, the EDA capitalized revolving loan funds under Title IX beginning in 1975. Community Development Block Grants (CDBGs) and Urban Development Action Grants (UDAGs) under HUD have also been used as sources for local loans or loan funds. UDAGs have been especially popular for use in conjunction with IRBs. UDAG participation has enabled clients to double the available size of the IRB to $20 million. Securing an additional $10 million loan at several points under the market rate saves a company a considerable amount of money over the term of the loan. Thus the UDAG carries a sizable premium to the company.

The most viable current sources of funds are CDBG, UDAG, and the SBA 503 program. Localities may access these sources to fund particular projects, and the loan repayments from these projects may be used to capitalize local business development funds.

The SBA 503 program offers fixed-asset financing to small businesses, the principal and interest of which is fully guaranteed by SBA.

The purpose of the program is to promote private investments that increase employment, business opportunities, and tax base in a locality. The 503 program requires the community to establish a local development corporation (LDC) which meets certain size and representation standards to become SBA certified. The LDC is usually established as a nonprofit entity, although for-profit entities are allowed. It may include representatives of business organizations, community organizations, private lenders, and local government. SBA requires representation from two of these four groups and a professional staff. Once certified, the LDC may offer up to $500,000 in debt capital for up to 25 years at about the long-term treasury bill rate in effect at closing. Funds are raised from the sale of guaranteed debentures. SBA sells the securities through the Federal Financing Bank.

The LDC can finance up to 50 percent of any project. To complete the financing, the LDC may make a 10 percent investment in the project using local resources instead of or in addition to an equity contribution from the investor(s). A private lender usually provides the remaining financing. The LDC is set up as a permanent entity, but the SBA financing is provided on a project-by-project basis.

Any SBA-qualified small business may apply for financing. The funds can be used to acquire fixed assets, including land, or to cover the construction costs incurred building or rehabilitating plant and facilities. Funds cannot be used for working capital or refinancing.

The LDC usually lends the funds to the eligible small business which in turn constructs or purchases the fixed assets. The LDC can also make assets available by selling property it owns to the business or by leasing property to the business either on a straight lease or under a lease-purchase arrangement.

The UDAG program can be applied to business development, real estate development, or industrial development projects in distressed urban areas. Funds can be used for public facilities and infrastructure, site improvements, building construction or rehabilitation, machinery and equipment purchases, and other fixed assets. As under the 503 program, funds cannot be used for working capital or refinancing. Local governments provide funds to private businesses in the form of loans, interest subsidies, lease financing, or even equity infusions.

UDAG funds are divided into two pools: one for larger cities and one for smaller cities. HUD receives proposals from local jurisdictions and makes grant awards on a competitive basis. The locality usually lends UDAG funds to local developers or businesses, and the private debtors are obligated to repay principal and interest to the locality.

UDAG loans are quite flexible. Principal amount, term, interest rate, amortization schedule, and security arrangements are all negotiable. On the other hand, selection criteria and participant commitment requirements are very specific. These are given in Appendix C.

Finally, the CDBG program channels funds to larger cities on an entitlement basis and to other localities through state governments or HUD. The monies are used differently from place to place and for a wide variety of community development purposes. Therefore the many possibilities are difficult to summarize. CDBG funds are used to capitalize directly local loan funds in some places. Elsewhere the funds are allocated competitively to local economic and community development projects. Frequently the criteria and structure of the UDAG program provide the model and guidelines.

For example, North Carolina administers the Small Cities CDBG program. Except for the 15 largest North Carolina cities, all cities, towns, and counties are eligible to compete for funding. About 20 percent of the funds are applied to economic development projects. Selected projects must result directly in the creation or retention of permanent employment opportunities and essential services in eligible communities, benefit primarily low- and moderate-income residents of those communities, provide leverage of private and other public funds, and require the proposed amount of CDBG funds for success.

The state allows CDBG funds to be used flexibly to finance any combination of fixed or current assets. Term, interest rate, amortization, and security are variable and justified in the context of the particular project. Principal is limited to $750,000. The debt capital is available to help start, expand, or acquire businesses that create or retain jobs. CDBG funds can also be used to provide public facilities or infrastructure to support business expansions.

Since these nonlocal sources of capitalization may not prove adequate, local actors should be prepared to request contributions from local sources. To attract local funds, several significant problems must be overcome. Most importantly, a clear, concise, and operational strategy of local economic development is an absolute necessity. Without clear guidelines, local investors will not be attracted, and financing requests will not be evaluated objectively. The latter situation could lead to the financing of inferior projects at best or, at worst, suits against the local funding agency. Those business entities denied financing could claim that the agency used arbitrary criteria and procedures in allocating funds. Business development, defined simply as the expansion or retention of local employment opportunities, is not a concept sufficiently precise to avoid legal and administrative problems in many instances. This problem is confounded by current economic conditions. With real interest rates, business start-up rates, and bankruptcy rates at historic highs, a financing program offering favorable terms will be very popular indeed. Objective criteria and even-handed procedures will be needed to establish credibility and to permit a high proportion of all financing requests to be rejected.

The second problem is the converse of the excess demand problem. Identifying many strong financing prospects, particularly in smaller communities or urban sub-areas, may be difficult. In these instances, the fund should be established at a citywide, regional, or even statewide level in order to deepen the pool of attractive projects. This regional approach has other advantages as well. First, competent administration of the fund is an absolute necessity, and many areas often cannot generate enough business to hire a capable fund administrator. Next, a larger fund will reduce the relative importance of any single project and therefore lower the impact of default associated with any one debtor. This larger, more diversified portfolio of projects may lower nonsystematic risk and risk associated with the particular location. Finally, a pool of funds for a larger geographic area will reduce the effects of parochial interests and local politics on the evaluation and selection process.

Assuming that a city, county, group of counties, or state containing at least several hundred thousand people agreed to start a business development fund, the initial capitalization will depend upon the degree of local support for the idea. Local persons who agree with the fund's purposes and have confidence in its administrators can become contributors to the fund. A fund prospectus that is competently done should attract local support by serving as an effective marketing instrument. The main features of the fund should be described concisely. Considerable attention should be devoted to the style, format, and design of the document.

The most likely institutional sources of funds include local branches of statewide banks, local thrifts and credit unions, major employers, and local foundations. The best strategy is starting with the most prestigious concerns and best-known financiers to request modest contributions to the fund. The remaining prospects are approached next. Even nominal contributions should be solicited. The broader the local base of support, the better. Finally, the largest prospects should be contacted again and asked to provide any remaining difference between the target amount and the amount pledged.

The second phase involves contacting individuals. A similar strategy should be followed: contact wealthy individuals and local leaders first; then solicit contributions from the community at large. The funds can also be organized in a way to make individual and corporate contributions tax-exempt.

Due to recent changes in banking and tax laws, individuals have a much wider choice of savings vehicles. Besides having tax-deferred annuities, certificates of deposit (CDs), and money market funds, even moderate-income individuals are starting individual retirement accounts (IRAs) and family trusts. They may be willing to deposit a small percentage of these long-term savings in local development funds that paid modest interest rates. The annual capitalization potential from local sources is significant even if very conservative assumptions are made. For example, an area with only 200,000 people and average per capita income of under $7,000 typically generates at least $65 million in annual savings. A fund accessing 1 percent of that amount for five years will have an impressive $3.2 million in capitalization.

If these capitalization strategies appear infeasible, a demonstration approach should be considered as an alternative. Local actors should design a local project involving the financing of a local business and develop the project proposal under one of the federal or state financing programs. If the proposal is funded, the local fund is set up to extend the loan to the business and to administer the loan repayment process. After one or two successful projects, the local fund administrator should be in a position to approach local sources for contributions and deposits, having demonstrated the potential of business development financing to most area residents.

MANAGING LOCAL BUSINESS DEVELOPMENT FUNDS

The adequately capitalized local economic development fund must also be well managed. The staff must be supported by local leaders and have an honest commitment to the area. Beyond committed and capable personnel, clear objectives to guide the allocation of development funds are crucial, as noted above. The objectives of job creation and retention will often be too broad to provide a satisfactory basis for discriminating between competing uses of funds. Fund managers may well have to introduce additional *economic* development concerns in order to promote effectively *business* development strategies.

As noted in Chapter 3, we have no widely accepted theory of economic development upon which to formulate a set of "correct" economic development objectives. Yet the public sector has the right and the responsibility to define its *own* indicators of risk and reward in the realm of economic development. Localities should array their projects in a risk–reward space that they have defined to determine their optimum project portfolios. The possibility of public–private partnerships exists as long as there is an overlap between projects that are attractive to both public and private sectors although each may use different definitions of reward and risk to make project selections. One way to examine alternative objectives is to introduce a series of specific economic development objectives and simulate the impact of each on the allocation of economic development funds among several local projects. Candidate objectives to be added to the objectives of job creation and retention are as follows: permanence of employment over time; quality of employment in terms of wages, hours, working conditions, fringe benefits, job security, and career mobility; stability of employment both seasonally and over the business cycle; the growth characteristics of the industry in which the employment is located; and quality of management in terms of commitment to the area, basic competence, and authority to make planning decisions.

Establishing eligibility requirements may also be useful. Minimums or maximums may be set with respect to establishment size, age of firm, experience of management, or prevailing wage rates. Financing may be limited to business starts, acquisitions, or expansions. Local contract construction, personal services, and certain retail trade sectors may be made ineligible to avoid antagonizing competitors that did not receive financing. Dealing only with locally owned firms, firms with fewer than a given number of employees, or firms committed to expanding operations locally may prove wise.

Finally, the firm's history of creating and maintaining employment in the area may be an important consideration.[2] (See Exercise 8.)

Objectives and eligibility requirements considered in the risk–reward framework should provide a sound basis for administering the fund. A direct, logical connection should be made between business development objectives, allowable uses of funds, eligibility standards, and funding requirements. If diverse objectives are established, set up separate accounts for each priority and figure out how much money should be assigned to each account. For example, one fund for job creation, another for job retention. Some objectives may require an equity capital fund, while others may require debt capital.

To acquire expertise for managing local economic development funds effectively, local talent should be called upon for help. Officers of a local financial institution or a consortium of financial institutions should be asked to help establish and assist in the administration of the fund.

To determine the best uses of funds, fund directors should seek situations in which private sources commit equity capital and debt capital. In fact they should require that some minimum percentage of the required financing be provided by owners/investors and private lenders before considering any infusion of public funds. In addition to degree of private participation, they should determine which financial vehicles and instruments will be offered.

The local business development fund can offer grants, equity capital, debt capital, in-kind contributions, leased assets, or guarantees. Grants are not recommended in general because businesses should be viable enough to repay the public sector for financial assistance. Although they have worked to encourage successful projects in some communities, grants more often have been extracted from the public by businesses threatening to leave an area or to invest elsewhere. Some localities may be able to justify grants in terms of greater tax revenues, net of public expenditures, derived either directly or indirectly from the project. However, these arguments in favor of grants are not easily justified for business development funds seeking involvement in viable joint ventures. Moreover, the fund will not last long if grants are allowed.

Fund directors should facilitate private in-kind contributions to joint projects. In-kind contributions are preferable to grants because they achieve the same end without tying up the fund's money or credit. The most typical in-kind contribution from the public sector is land donated to a developer to instigate a project. Again, if public–private projects are economically viable, the business development fund should be able to arrange some form of pay-back. Assets directly provided to a project should represent a loan, not a grant, whenever possible.

Leasing, either as part of lease-purchase arrangements or sale-leaseback arrangements, has received much attention recently. However, recent and proposed changes in the tax laws make it difficult to offer general guidelines. In the past, communities have constructed facilities and leased them to businesses either under a straight lease or lease-purchase arrangement. Because accountants treat long-term leases as debt, leases will not be discussed separately but subsumed under the discussion of debt instruments.

The public sector has made equity investments in private companies. The federal government's participation in the refinancing of major corporations and banks is well known. Arguments exist in favor of providing equity capital for business development from public sources as a way of exerting more influence on the direction of the business. Indeed, CDBGs and UDAGs may be used this way. However, this influence is more illusory than real when the public sector represents a minority ownership interest. Moreover, the liquidity of the equity investment is low unless the company is a large public corporation with stock that is actively traded on one of the major exchanges.

In general, the development fund should be very reluctant to offer equity capital, even if the public sector were encouraged to take an equity position in a profit-making business. First, the responsibility for success and failure should rest with the individuals who own and manage the business, and they alone should reap the rewards or suffer the losses. Assuming such risks is inappropriate for the public because the private investors should be willing to do so. Second, designing sound ways of calling equity investments that would neither harm the financial position of the business nor reduce the liquidity of the fund will be difficult. This dilemma is sometimes called the venture capital problem. Third, competing with national venture capital funds, small business investment companies (SBICs), or informal sources of equity capital is unproductive. Doing so unnecessarily reduces the capitalization of the fund by displacing private investment. Fourth, separating the interests of the fund from those of the businesses seeking financing is prudent. This separation helps ensure arm's length transactions that enhance the local credibility of the fund over the long term. Finally and most importantly, most of the benefits of equity instruments can be offered by structuring debt instruments in flexible and ingenious ways.

On the other hand, debt instruments offered with standard terms and conditions will not be helpful in most situations. This type of straight debt financing is available from commercial banks and other private sources of financing. It is unlikely to alter private risks and returns significantly or help achieve business development objectives.

In general, the business development fund should consider flexible debt instruments and loan guarantees. Subordinated debt financing in the form of loans or notes and carrying favorable terms is one recommended alternative. The security of the fund's debt is subordinated to the private creditor's security. This instrument can combine important advantages of equity capital and debt capital. Like equity capital, subordinated loans are flexible enough to supplement other forms of financing. For example, if the bank were unwilling to commit a loan beyond 5 or 7 years, a subordinated loan could provide long-term, fixed-asset financing. Such loans can sometimes access private financing on more favorable terms. Because the subordinated loan lowers bank exposure, commercial financing may be secured for a longer term or at lower cost. Lower interest rates also improve the bank's position by increasing the profitability and cash flow of the business.

More importantly, the development fund may be in a position to provide "patient money" to the business by requiring low periodic payments during the early years and higher payments later (graduated amortization). Ways to structure flexible loan amortization schedules in combination with variable or fixed interest rates to support business development are indeed numerous. (Financing principles are discussed in Chapter 6.)

As a form of debt capital, subordinated loans neither dilute ownership nor complicate the control of the business. The established amortization schedule eliminates the venture capital problem.

Subordinated loans can also carry below-market interest rates which improve private returns and reduce the risk to private investors. The degree of interest subsidy should vary with the extent to which the uses of funds were expected to achieve economic or business development objectives. For example, a business offering more jobs or better jobs per dollar of public investment should be eligible for lower interest rates than the norm.

Subordinated debt capital is no panacea, however. The local economic development fund may not be able to recover its investment in cases of business failure, and it may not want to foreclose on problem loans given its business development mission of job creation and retention. Yet the fund must recover its capital to remain viable. Thus we must consider ways to address the default problem. The fund should try to secure a lien on a general asset such as land instead of specific assets of the business for which there are narrow, shallow, or fragmented markets. In this regard, business development projects involving real estate may be preferable because liens on land and structures (general assets) represent better security than liens on other current or fixed business assets. An ample loan loss reserve can be established or insurance purchased, but these options are expensive and tie up funds. Obviously, more than adequate collateral affords some protection. Yet excessive collateral requirements and extensive personal guarantees can be burdensome to the businesses seeking financing and can discourage entrepreneurship.

Another funding vehicle is senior debt capital made available with the same flexibility as subordinated debt but giving the fund a first security position on the relevant business assets. Loans that are a senior lien on assets should be the norm when seller financing is available or no other lenders are involved. To the extent that the fund is financing acquisitions, some seller financing should be required. Furthermore, seller financing has tactical merit by giving former owners a stake in the success of the business that they sell.

In most instances, debt instruments will be structured as a loan from the development fund to business owners. In other instances, the business will want to sell bonds to local investors either directly or through the fund. In circumstances, the business owners may be able to sell subordinated debentures to the fund on mutually attractive terms.[3] A development fund enjoying tax-exempt status, for example, is in a position to purchase deep-discount, zero coupon bonds from the business which, in turn, is able to realize lower financing costs and better terms with this instrument.

Another possible instrument to be offered by the fund is a loan guarantee. Guarantees insure a portion of the private lender's loans to businesses. By reducing the lender's risk and exposure, the guarantee encourages business loans that would otherwise not be made. For commercial banks and savings and loans, guarantees extend the lender's loan limit by the amount of the guarantee. In other words, a lender with a $200,000 loan limit could extend a loan in the amount of $1.0 million with an 80 percent guarantee.

Federal guarantees give lenders access to secondary markets. With SBA or FmHA guarantee programs, for example, private lenders are able to sell the guaranteed portion of the loan in national markets. With a guarantee from the local development fund, the lender will not have a national market available but may be able to solicit interest from the local investor community in the guaranteed loans.

The development fund should not offer a fixed guarantee but permit the portion to vary between limits of 20 percent to 80 percent. Given business development objectives, the guaranteed portion of the loan can be increased as the project becomes increasingly attractive. Going above 80 percent is not wise because some exposure for the private lender should be maintained to assure a careful credit analysis and to keep attention focused on the investment after the loan is closed. Although guarantees usually cover both outstanding principal and interest, principal-only guarantees are another alternative. Such guarantees are cheaper yet may still be attractive to local lenders.

Following the example of the federal guarantee programs, guarantee reserves should be fully funded. Less than fully funded reserves should be considered only for large funds managed by experienced personnel. This point underscores the importance of organizing the fund at a reasonable scale, possibly at the metropolitan, regional, or statewide level.

The major advantage of loan guarantees compared to direct loans lies in the leverage potential. The fund generates one dollar in loans with an 80¢ guarantee at most. The major disadvantages are less involvement in the project and less knowledge of the bank's assessment of the project. As guarantor, the fund stands as a third party behind the lender and, therefore, does not deal directly with the business.

Whichever instruments are applied, the local development fund's portfolio will be inherently riskier than those of private sector lenders, given its role as supporter of business development strategies in a particular geographic area. Therefore, committing only a portion of deposits to local investments is sensible. Part of the fund's portfolio should be placed in low-risk corporate or government securities. Although such investments cannot be overdone, they offer a way to lower the nonsystematic risks inherent in localized lending. The fund can also place deposits with regional or statewide banks with lending policies that are compatible with the fund's business development objectives.

The fund should sustain a positive cash flow after meeting administrative expenses. Without fresh capitalization, new loan commitments will depend on the rate at which previous loans are repaid. Indeed, a small revolving loan fund may make a spate of initial loans and then become inactive for many years waiting for these loans to be repaid. Assuming that fresh funds cannot be secured frequently and that some portion of loans will be long-term, cash flow of the fund may be increased by creating a secondary market for its securities (assets), that is, the loans or guarantees discussed above. One idea is to find a purchaser of the total or guaranteed portion of these loans among local investment trusts, pension funds, insurance companies, or other intermediaries with medium to long-term liability structures. Transaction costs can be minimized by describing the loan portfolio to portfolio managers and offering to continue loan servicing for a modest fee. However, subordinated loans will have to be offered at a discount to get a serious response from private fund managers. The development fund will have to establish a good track record before a secondary market for its securities can be established.

From a process perspective, local actors should think about building the business development fund in stages. In localities without prior experience in development finance, nonlocal grant funds should be tapped to offer loans to finance local business expansions only. In the next stage, local contributions should be forthcoming and added to repayments from loans made earlier, as confidence in fund management increased. As the fund moves toward full capitalization, contributions should be invested in low-risk, liquid securities such as CDs purchased through local and regional financial intermediaries. In the fourth stage, expansions and other types of business development projects should be considered with loans or guarantees extended to the most competitive projects. Loan funds will be generated by liquidating short-term investments. However, some funds will remain as investments to lower risk to some degree. After gaining a good reputation, the fund may be able to replenish its resources by selling loans to local investors at a discount. In the final stage, the fund may accept deposits and establish savings accounts or share accounts that earn interest. The fund will have to pay lower rates of interest to depositors to avoid potential competition with private lenders and to reflect the fact that its portfolio was not earning interest at market rates.

Local actors should seriously consider the financing requirements of local business development strategies. The particulars will vary from place to place, but successful local business development funds should have sufficient geographic coverage, broadly based local support, cooperation from local financial institutions, clear and precise objectives and procedures for evaluating applications for financing, flexible debt instruments, and possibly a secondary market for recapitalization.[4] For further discussion, see the readings on development finance. (See Exercise 9.)

In the next four chapters, we move from the general, strategic level to the project level where we consider the planning and execution of business development and real estate development projects. Because we have dealt with strategic issues in the first four chapters, we should be able to see projects as part of a coherent, reinforcing, and cumulative process that promotes local economic development. As a review, readers should test themselves to be sure that they can answer the following four questions with confidence:

1. How do you define economic development for the perspective of the aims, resources, strengths and weaknesses of the organization with which you are affiliated?
2. Which economic development strategies or, more narrowly, business development strategies are most in tune with your organization's strategic interests and with the concerns of most local officials, businesspersons, bankers, workers, and key local actors?
3. How do you define your organization's role in the economic development process given the local situation? Which tools will you utilize to implement your economic/business development strategies? How will you get others to do their part? How will you pay for the planning efforts?
4. How will you raise funds for economic or business development strategies? Which objectives, rules, and criteria will you establish for the fund? Which financial instrument(s) will you employ?

Please review Exercises 1–9 in considering these questions.

NOTES

1. Nominal interest rates are thought to reflect a real rate of interest, an inflation premium, and a risk premium. Thus rising nominal interest rates with constant real rates of interest occur during periods of inflation or as the degree of perceived risk increases. Interest-rate differentials between tax-exempt markets (where general obligation bonds and revenue bonds are exchanged) and other capital markets have narrowed in recent years. The narrowing is *partly* attributed to the greater riskiness of tax-exempt bonds, which carry a higher risk premium as a result.

2. A framework borrowed from linear programming may be quite helpful. First, specify the objectives and constraints to be used as project evaluation criteria. Ideally, each objective should derive from a serious discussion of local economic development issues. Each should be measured quantitatively and weighted to account for its importance relative to other objectives. Together, the objectives represent the social returns anticipated from development investing (see Figure 4). The constraints reflect private returns and commercial feasibility, either establishing minimum expected return on private investment or maximum levels of risk. Other constraints can be used to indicate eligibility requirements and limits on funding for any single project. Identified projects should be rank-ordered by applying the rule of maximizing economic development objectives subject to the private risk/reward constraints.

The explicit framework dovetails nicely with the recommended administrative arrangements. If local fund directors join forces with a local financial institution or consortium of institutions to administer the fund, joint screening of potential projects will proceed as follows. Financial officers will receive proposed projects and apply previously accepted risk/reward criteria to appraise each project (the constraints). Fund staff will measure the project's social risk and contribution to economic development objectives. A priority list of projects will be jointly established. As experience grows, the objectives, weights, and constraints will be sharpened periodically.

3. Subordinated debentures are debt instruments issued by a business that are generally unsecured and frequently convertible to common or preferred equity.

4. The finance terms used in this chapter are defined in Chapter 6.

5

LOCAL ECONOMIC
DEVELOPMENT PROJECTS

A project is an organized undertaking designed to get something done. What qualifies as an economic development project depends on the understanding of the economic development process that local actors share. If strategic or contingency planning is successful, it should be relatively easy to describe the characteristics of local economic development projects, at least in general terms. The discussion of business development in Chapter 3 suggests that business starts, expansions, and acquisitions qualify as economic development projects when job creation and retention are major goals. In addition to job creation, concern with the local tax base has led many communities to embrace commercial and neighborhood revitalization projects as an important part of economic development. Here nonresidential real estate projects are included in the category of relevant economic development projects. With respect to jobs and tax base objectives, business development projects have a direct impact on jobs and a more indirect impact on the tax base. Conversely commercial and industrial real estate projects directly affect the tax base and, by providing space for employers, have an indirect impact on jobs.

While most business and real estate projects are privately initiated, the jobs and tax base objectives can be furthered by projects involving the public sector. Enterprise development projects include private business development projects, public enterprise development projects, and public–private enterprise development projects (or simply, public–private ventures). Co-development projects connote active public-sector involvement in real estate development projects. Finally, traditional public investments that create public facilities and infrastructure remain essential to promoting local economic development because they are needed to create the proper environment for business and real estate development. While included in the category of economic development projects, public investments are de-emphasized to focus attention on profit-oriented and revenue-generating projects. However, the process described below applies to these projects as well. Furthermore, the proper relationship between traditional public investments and emerging public–private projects is an important issue in its own right and one that is discussed subsequently.

Project planning is a process that is described briefly in Chapter 2 as part of contingency planning. The process is presented more fully in the next section of this chapter. The rest of this chapter describes specific stages of the project planning phase, namely project organization, evaluation, identification, and formulation.

THE PROJECT PLANNING AND MANAGEMENT CYCLE

Project planning is the first phase of the project planning and management cycle. As shown in Figure 5, this project cycle may be divided into the following steps or stages: organization, identification, formulation, design, financing, appraisal and approval, activation, implementation, completion, normal operations, and evaluation. The cycle notion suggests a circular movement linking the planning phase and management phase. While individual projects are discrete, the planning phase is continuous. In other words, an economic development project is planned, executed, and subsequently spun off to become a viable, ongoing activity. However, the cycle continues with consideration of the next set of projects. The planning phase is comprised of evaluation, organization, identification, formulation, design, financing, appraisal and approval, and activation; the management phase begins with activation and ends with evaluation, indicating a necessary overlap between project planning and project management. The management phase may be further broken down into a developmental phase and an operational phase which also overlap. The former consists of activation, implementation, and completion; the latter consists of completion, normal operations, and evaluation.

FIG. 5. Phases of the Project-Planning and Management Cycle

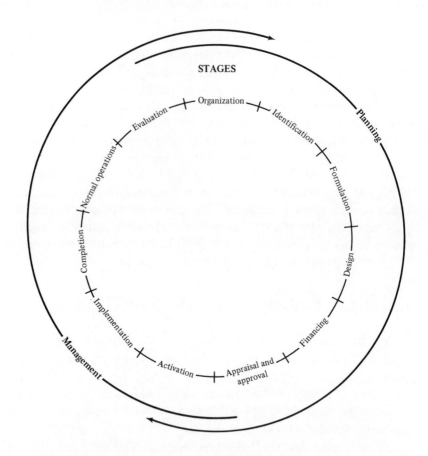

We may describe the contributions of various actors in the project planning and management cycle in order to connect the people doing planning and management as described in Chapter 1 to the steps of the project cycle. We may describe the persons who come up with the project idea as "entrepreneurs," the persons that design and evaluate the project as "technicians," the persons that finance the project as "financiers," the group that carries out the project as "contractors," the persons who take over the project to initiate normal operations as "managers," and the persons who evaluate and organize the project as "organizers." We may further divide the financiers' activities between the "investors" who put up equity capital and the "bankers" who provide the debt capital. For simplicity we may assume a correspondence between these actors and each stage of the project cycle in which they play a leading role, as follows: entrepreneurs/identification, entrepreneurs/formulation, technicians/design, entrepreneurs, investors, and bankers/financing, bankers/appraisal and approval, entrepreneurs and contractors/activation, contractors/implementation, contractors and managers/completion, managers/normal operations, technicians/evaluation, and organizers/organization.

Given this framework, how can local public actors enhance the success of local development projects? They should assume one of three roles throughout the project cycle: leader, partner, or facilitator. Local elected officials and community leaders should assume a lead role in organizing the relevant actors in the first place, especially when local economic development is approached as a joint private-public activity involving representatives of public agencies, private organizations, and community groups. LDO directors and professional staff should join entrepreneurs as partners in the identification and formulation of particular development projects. They should facilitate the detailed design and appraisal–approval stages and assume a more active partnership role during the project financing stage. They typically act as facilitators during activation, have no role in implementation, completion, or normal operations and again assume a lead role in project evaluation. To be effective in their public leadership and partnership roles, local actors should have a clear understanding of what is involved in project evaluation, organization, identification, formulation, and financing. We will elaborate these roles in this and the following chapters.

During project organization, local leaders must establish the network capable of supporting projects in creative ways and identify the persons willing to plan and manage particular projects that contribute to local economic development. These are the lead organizations and key actors that should be involved in strategic and contingency planning as discussed in Chapter 2 and in designing and financing local economic development as discussed in Chapters 3 and 4.

During project evaluation, LDO professionals assess the realized or proposed project and judge its expected impact on local economic development. They ask, exactly how has/will this project enhance(d) local economic development? Obviously, the strategic perspectives covered in the previous four chapters should be quite valuable in evaluating particular projects. During project identification, they

TABLE 5. The Project-Planning and Management Cycle

Stage	Major tasks	Local economic development professional	
		Role	Functions
Organization	Create organizational network	Lead	Identify key individuals and organizations
			Present scenarios on important economic events, describe relevant local plans and related policies, arrange meetings, etc.
	Facilitate entrepreneurship		Help identify and negotiate with prospective entrepreneurs
	Organize supportive functions		Mobilize supportive services needed for project initiation
Identification	Define economic development projects	Partner with entrepreneurs	Involve local persons with project ideas
			Identify and describe project ideas
	Assess project in terms of economic development potential, risk, and return		Do preliminary check against economic development objectives and criteria
			Help prepare project justification
Formulation	Refine and improve project ideas	Partner with entrepreneurs	Determine political feasibility
			Secure political support for project from local influentials

(continued)

84

TABLE 5 (continued)

| Stage | Major tasks | Local economic development professional | |
		Role	Functions
[Formulation]			Arrange outside review of project's economic and operational feasibility
			Help identify local expertise to examine the financing plan
			Review all formal feasibility studies
Design	Complete engineering and architectural plans	Facilitator	Help arrange engineering, architectural, and legal services
	Prepare legal documents		
	Prepare project implementation schedule and workplan		Help outline project implementation plan
Financing	Arrange equity financing	Partner with entrepreneurs and financiers	Consider innovative methods of equity financing
			Facilitate agreement on ownership structure and profit participation
	Secure debt financing		Help locate potential sources of debt financing
			Apply to public sources of financing
Appraisal and approval	Gain financial approvals for the project	Facilitator	Help provide additional information about the project

(continued)

TABLE 5 (continued)

| Stage | Major tasks | Local economic development professional | |
		Role	Functions
[Appraisal and approval]	Gain necessary government approvals		Help obtain formal approval from public agencies
Activation	Request and review bids for construction work, if any	Facilitator	Help review bids
	Select project contractor		
	Recruit project work force		Troubleshoot to reduce delays
Implementation	Construct facilities or mobilize assets		
	Set up machinery, equipment, and internal spaces		
	Train personnel		
Completion	Begin selling product or leasing space		
	Transfer operations to line managers		
	Repay construction financing, if any		
Normal operations	Begin full-capacity operations		
	Establish operations and maintenance procedures		
	Set up accounting, comptroller, and other management control functions		

(continued)

TABLE 5 (continued)

| Stage | Major tasks | Local economic development professional | |
		Role	Functions
Evaluation	Establish specific evaluation criteria	Lead	Specify evaluation methodology
	Assess actual perform-ance of economic development project		Collect information on project
			Compare performance to expectations
			Prepare evaluation report

Source: Compiled by author.

work with others to come up with practical and socially useful ideas for local economic development projects. Thinking about project evaluation should enhance the local capacity to identify effective economic development projects.

The feasibility of the project is determined during the project formulation stage. In shaping the project to improve its chances of success, political, operational, and economic feasibility are considered.

Project financing involves finding the sources and determining the specific methods of paying for the activities needed to activate and implement the project and for the assets required to start normal operations.

In Table 5, the major activities for each of the eleven stages of the project cycle are summarized. Lead, partner, and facilitator roles of LDO professionals are also outlined. (See Baum 1970, 1978; Rondinelli 1977.)

PROJECT ORGANIZATION

As noted in Chapter 3, an organizational network is needed to foster joint private–public projects that promote business development. An organizational network is equally useful in creating the local basis for pursuing any aspect of economic development. A local development organization formally responsible for area-wide economic development would be in the best position to take a leadership role in project organization. LDO directors should identify and bring together the key actors needed to discuss ideas for joint projects. These key actors may be organized as subcommittees of the local economic development entity, as a separate task force or working group, or as an advisory group to the entity and to other public agencies. Of course effective contingency planning and strategic planning will greatly facilitate project organization.

LDO directors should spend a good deal of time and effort to promote a sense of long-term commitment and of sharing burdens and responsibilities for local economic development activities. At the same time, they should outline priorities and stress the need to achieve tangible results in the short term. As specific project ideas are considered, they should solicit the names of persons who could assume lead responsibility for project planning and management. Promising matches between lead persons and project ideas must be found. These lead persons should be asked to assume the entrepreneurial roles required for project execution. If the selection process works properly, the entrepreneurs should be individuals that are concerned both with achieving local economic development opportunities and with gaining personal financial rewards. The combination of community service and profit motivations will strengthen commitments to local projects.

Many individuals and organizational representatives who give casual support to a project idea originally may withdraw their support when the project idea has a chance to become a reality. LDO directors need to find out how strongly key individuals and economic development task force members actually support an identified project. Through these discussions, not only is the effectiveness of project organization being tested, but the political feasibility of project ideas is also being considered.

LDO directors should seek explicit verbal commitments and informal agreements from the key actors, because it is far too cumbersome to proceed on any other basis. This approach underscores the importance of being explicit about expectations and dealing with people who are trustworthy.

Most effective economic development professionals follow common-sense procedures to gain commitments and agreements. After identifying all of the important actors and sketching their roles in the project, they describe how each person could contribute to the success of the project. They seek an agreement with each person to carry out the anticipated tasks in a timely fashion and meet with everyone individually to iron out differences of opinion. The group is called together after basic agreements are reached.

Once the entrepreneurship function is fulfilled, the LDO director should be primarily concerned with technical assistance, capacity building (to improve project administration and to foster the generation of other local economic development projects), and project financing, when putting the project together. These tasks refer to the formulation, design, and financing stages of the project cycle. To carry out these tasks, the LDO is offering the basic business support services to promote economic development that venture capital groups, local business development organizations, and community development corporations offer to their clients.

At the project level, technical assistance involves formulating and packaging the project, careful sequencing of critical project milestones, arranging negotiations, and facilitating agreements. Without exaggeration these services are worth many thousands of dollars in terms of the time and effort required to successfully plan, initiate, and manage a local project.

Capacity building is the accumulated experience that develops within the organizational network from providing technical assistance. The organizational support given to one project gradually becomes a permanent apparatus for spawning other projects. Support is required in the fundamentals of business management, including marketing, accounting, finance, and business law. Capacity building is needed because it takes time to influence local economic development, which is a difficult, complex, and protracted process.

Financial support includes the ability to raise equity capital and access loans and loan guarantees. No local economic development project can survive without adequate financing. Finally, project evaluation provides the knowledge base that improves all project planning activities including technical assistance, capacity building, and financing.

PROJECT EVALUATION

Project evaluation can be completed at the beginning or end of the project cycle. LDO professionals require knowledge to screen initial project ideas and to assess the impact of executed projects. They must estimate how the project will contribute or has contributed to local economic development. There are several methods available for evaluating development projects. In most instances, these methods are proposed to select the "best" project(s) from a list of *proposed* projects. For our purposes, however, project evaluation refers more often to methods and procedures used to evaluate the *results* of a few good project ideas that have been carried out.

The most sophisticated method of project evaluation is benefit-cost analysis, which includes the modifications designed to account for multiple objectives. The approach has great merit for large-scale development projects and has been used to evaluate U.S. development projects, particularly in water resources development. Unfortunately, most local officials view the approach as too complicated, expensive, and time consuming for evaluating smaller-scale projects. However, there is a more profound reason why benefit-cost analysis is seldom used. Implicit in the benefit-cost framework is a definition of economic development that is not widely accepted in U.S. localities.[1]

Regardless of its level of acceptance, benefit-cost analysis offers a powerful tool for project evaluation which is appropriate in most cases. It provides a clear framework for sorting out project inputs and outputs and distinguishing among benefits and costs. It forces the evaluator to relate the outcomes of a particular project to the more general social objectives to be served. It gives an explicit way to choose among alternative uses of limited public resources.

Benefit-cost analysis also requires that society be defined. Does society comprise the citizens of the locality, state, nation, or world? Most local economic development is practiced as if each locality were a separate society. Because of this attitude, local economic development practice is often parochial and mercantile and fails to consider overall economic well-being. Thus the benefit-cost framework deserves to be considered seriously.

There are alternatives to benefit-cost analysis. Cost-effectiveness analysis compares the opportunity costs of achieving a particular level of output. It is less complex than cost-benefit analysis because it avoids the difficulties of measuring social benefits. The approach can be used to do comparative cost analyses of alternative industrial complexes, redevelopment projects, or any development projects with similar outcomes. Other techniques adapt cash flow analysis. Fiscal impact analysis, for example, measures the direct tax revenues and expenditures generated by local development projects. It avoids the issue of defining society by focusing on the local government as a corporate entity. Only cash inflows and outlays of this entity are taken into account. Other methods are used for selecting capital improvement projects. (See Sugden and Williams 1978; Vogt 1977.)

Three common techniques for comparing different streams of cash flow over time are net present value, internal rate of return, and payback period. The payback approach is the simplest. Cash outlays at one point in time are compared to cash returns from those outlays received over time. The project restoring outlays in the shortest period of time is the best project. Internal rate of return calculates the return on income generated by the project. The highest rate of return indicates the best project. Net present value discounts income and outlay streams to the present time period and takes the difference between the present values. The project with the highest net income is best. Net present value is the most accurate technique.[2]

The approach suggested here attempts to conform to the spirit of the benefit-cost framework but is more qualitative and less precise. It involves use of an economic development checklist. The definition of local economic development accepted by the community can be posed as a series of questions asked of a particular development project. (Review Exercise 5.) Thus the economic development checklist is constructed as a detailed definition of local economic development cast in terms that are relevant at the project level. As the checklist is used repeatedly to evaluate projects, LDO staff should learn more and more about the complexities and dynamics of local economic development.

The economic development checklist is shown in Table 6. The questions are phrased in ex ante terms (that is, as if the evaluation were to take place before project activation). They may be easily changed to evaluate projects after implementation.

The checklist is rather long. No priority is assigned either to major categories or to specific questions. The checklist should be adapted to each local situation. First, different weights should be assigned to the major categories such as making the project impact

TABLE 6. Economic Development Checklist

Impacts

Would the project expand or improve the productive capacity of the local economy or would it simply result in changes of ownership or control?

Would the project make a contribution to the *national* economy or would it result in local gains at the expense of other areas?

Would the project result in the elimination of local jobs, the reduction of local sales, or the increase of local public expenditures?

Taking the answers to the previous question into account, would the project increase local jobs, sales, or tax revenues on a net basis?

To what extent would employment and business opportunities resulting from the project accrue to local residents? To economically disadvantaged persons?

Would the project provide better-paying jobs, better working conditions (in terms of hours, seasonal stability, fringe benefits, health and safety of the work place, etc.), better career advancement possibilities (incentives, job ladders), or more permanent jobs compared to existing employment opportunities?

Would the project have favorable or unfavorable impacts on the local natural environment? On prime agricultural land?

Would the project have positive or negative impacts on the local quality of life?

Would the project create capital gains and losses or otherwise impact on the distribution of wealth?

Outputs

Would the project develop new products, make better goods and services available, or produce more goods and services at lower prices?

Would the project result in commodities for export or for local consumption?

Would the project sell products to growing local/national markets?

Would the project generate any environmental pollutants or serious pollution problems?

Process

Would the project create a new company or be part of a growth industry?

To what extent is production expected to be cyclical or seasonal?

Would the project use new technology or rely on standard practice?

(continued)

TABLE 6 (continued)

[Process]

Would the project create innovative management practices or traditional ones, involve work rules or union representation?

Would the proposed management team have appropriate training and experience?

Inputs

Would renewable or nonrenewable natural resources be used? Would the project deplete nonrenewable resources?

Would material inputs and capital equipment be locally purchased or imported?

Would local workers be hired? How many?

Would job training be required? What kind?

Would input purchases stimulate local innovation or business development?

Construction of capacity (creating the assets)

How much construction activity would be required (in dollars)? How long is the construction period?

How many construction jobs would be generated? How many local workers would be hired?

How much subcontracting would go to local construction or professional firms (in dollars)?

Ownership of capacity

Would the capacity be locally owned? Absentee owned? Managed by locals? Publicly or privately held?

Would the capacity be an independent entity or a subsidiary or branch plant?

Would the workers participate in stock ownership or in management decisions?

Would local financial intermediaries own any debt or otherwise be involved in financing the project?

Source: Compiled by author.

category twice as important as any other category. Weighting specific questions in the checklist is also suggested. Questions that are irrelevant in a particular locality should be eliminated. (In other words, these questions are given zero weights.) Questions can be sharpened or added to reflect specific economic realities faced by the community.

The questions in the checklist can be answered with yes or no responses, simple numerical estimates, or a few ordinal scores. Scores can be added to get a rough estimate of the project's overall contribution to local economic development. The purpose of numerical scoring is to clarify the project's overall significance to local economic development. (See Exercise 10.)

PROJECT IDENTIFICATION

Project identification is the most essential yet most difficult activity in the project cycle. Generating good project ideas is central to the exercise of entrepreneurship and to the ability to seize local opportunities. Contingency and strategic planning provide frameworks for project identification in the context of specific environmental or contingent events. To improve the ability to generate alternative development projects, guidelines to identify economic development projects are offered below, and "model" economic development projects are presented subsequently.

Guidelines

In essence identifying economic development projects is a practical design activity. It is a design task because the aim is to apply one's creativity to come up with many alternative projects. The task must also be practical because compromises and trade-offs are required. Projects that improve people's well-being, increase productivity and economic viability, and enhance the quality of life and work may lack sufficient resources to be initiated, or the markets to sustain them. Trade-offs between meeting local development needs and making money are required. Unprofitable projects should be avoided. An acceptable cash flow should be sought.

Project identification is a creative process. Projects will not necessarily be discovered by knowing alternative theories of local economic development or by subjecting the local economy to rigorous quantitative analysis. Knowing the history and current status of the local economy in great detail will be helpful but not sufficient for generating project ideas.

Creative thinking will be discouraged if it is restricted to the economic development program categories supported by federal or state funding, regardless of the current status of that funding. The best sources of project ideas are people with shared concerns working through the local development organization, as are successful economic development projects tried in other communities.

The project identification process is working well when innovative ideas are forthcoming. Innovations usually arise as a response to a particular problem or difficult situation, following the adage that necessity is the mother of invention. For localities facing severe threats and dire economic contingencies, new workable economic arrangements, new applications of social inventions, and more entrepreneurship are needed. Consistent with the discussion of entrepreneurship in Chapter 3, a schema for classifying forms of entrepreneurship is given below that shows innovative project outcomes:

- Create new products (goods or services)
- Establish new markets for existing products
- Utilize new types or sources of inputs (natural resources, processed materials, equipment or facilities, transportation, communications, or worker skills)
- Introduce new techniques of production (ways to improve the productivity of the production process)
- Introduce new techniques of planning, management, administration, or sales (ways to improve the productivity of the organizational control process)

The remaining guidelines are keyed to these five potential outcomes:

New Products

Identifying new goods or services is the most difficult form of innovation. Many talented businesspersons devote their energies to this endeavor with little to show for their efforts. LDO staff should bring a somewhat different orientation to this activity. Instead of looking first at effective demand, the needs of the local population should be addressed by asking questions such as the following: What product can improve people's nutrition, health, education, or comfort? What product can improve the quality of the natural and working environments? What product can help stabilize the local economy? What product can effectively utilize local natural resources? What product can uniquely combine locally available inputs or draw upon the unique capabilities of the local population?

Usually a new venture is called for to create a new product. Ideally, the venture will fill an economic niche, making a new product available that satisfies demand, generating sufficient profits from sales to continue operations, and avoiding competition with other local companies. New venture creation requires a high level of expertise in particular industries and markets. For example, one LDO has been able to spawn several new ventures because of its in-depth knowledge of products derived from the dominant natural resource in its area.

New Markets

Identifying new markets is the easiest form of innovation. In many developing areas and developing countries, import substitution and export diversification are the basic strategies of economic development and represent strategies for creating new markets. To achieve import substitution, products are produced and sold locally that were currently being imported from outside the area. To achieve export diversification, local products are marketed in other areas.

In exploiting new markets, import substitution and export diversification projects should contribute to national as well as local economic development. They should increase aggregate output or improve the productivity of labor and capital rather than redistribute existing employment and industrial capacity.

One type of import substitution provides goods and services to local households and governments (final products); the other type sells commodities to local businesses (intermediate products). The LDO staff should try to identify local markets for both final and intermediate products, establish competitive standards of product quality, price, and service, and discuss new marketing possibilities with local businesspersons. The analysis can use formal information on interindustry sales and purchases and on market thresholds or rely on experiences and informal observations. The LDO should consider brokering contracts between local buyers and sellers.

Export diversification possibilities should be sought in a similar fashion. LDO staff should search for possibilities in growing regional or statewide markets and in underutilized industrial capacity, worker skills, or natural resources. Again, the cooperation of local businesses is essential to identify initial project possibilities.

New markets are usually exploited by expanding or retaining existing businesses rather than by starting new ones.

New Inputs and Techniques

Available local resources can suggest potential projects. Natural resources form the basis of potential agricultural, forestry, fishery, or mining projects. Renewable energy resources (wood, wind, and solar) can support new energy development projects. Existing buildings, equipment, or materials can be put to better use. For example, obsolete factory and warehouse facilities can be converted to industrial, commercial, or residential uses. Similarly, human resources are often unemployed or underemployed. One should ask, How could these local talents be used more developmentally? Are persons with good project ideas and business skills available to undertake new products?

Project possibilities should be sought through discussions with the owners of resources. Producer cooperatives are an effective way to organize the large number of small resource owners needed to initiate a project.

In seeking knowledge of new inventions and innovations, it is important to select technologies that put the available mix of local resources to effective use. The technology that is appropriate to an area should create jobs or improve productivity without significantly reducing employment opportunities or the quality of work. In some localities new fossil fuel conservation technologies are increasing employment while improving the quality of the workplace environment.

Introducing new techniques is often an important aspect of strategies to retain existing businesses.

New Organizational Forms

New production and organizational techniques are relevant to both growing and declining businesses. Growing businesses often require new management styles to accommodate growth. Declining businesses often shrink from internal management problems more than from external competition.

It may be possible to help diagnose the source of the business problem or at least to direct local businesses to available expertise and assistance. In some cases, substantial improvements can be made by introducing alternative organizational forms, especially when the decline results from intentional disinvestment or mismanagement. Alternative forms include producer cooperatives in either limited or full share ownership forms, community-owned and -managed firms, employee-owned or -managed firms, traditional partnerships, or S corporations.[3]

Organizational innovations have the potential of liberating the creative and productive energies of employees, supervisors, and management by changing their roles and relationships to give everyone a bigger stake in improving productivity and product quality.

Needless to say, these guidelines pose a very ambitious array of tasks for local actors seeking to identify economic development projects. Certainly, the guidelines should be modified and adapted to local conditions. In many places, expanding existing operations that are producing established products or acquiring viable existing businesses will be the most feasible projects. Although such projects are valid and legitimate, the guidelines are intended to raise the level of local economic development practice by focusing local actors' attention on innovation and by encouraging projects that contribute to national and local economic well-being. At present most economic development resources are being devoted to activities that improve local conditions at the cost of conditions in other areas. Considering positive-sum approaches like those proposed in this section is essential. Ultimately, constant- or zero-sum competition between areas is self-defeating. The first step in transcending the status quo is to present viable alternatives to local actors concerned with economic development.

Model Projects

Model projects are drawn from the experience of communities around the country. Some evolve in response to specific contingencies. Others are adaptations of projects tried elsewhere. We take a look at several common events and the related project ideas in this section of the chapter.

Practically every developmentally oriented community is prepared for a *new branch plant*. Usually the local government in conjunction with the industrial development agency has undertaken public works projects to create local infrastructure and has developed sites for industrial parks. The federal government, largely through FmHA and EDA, has underwritten these investments in the past.

When a branch plant is attracted to such an area, there is usually ample time to meet the site and services requirements of the proposed facility. Supportive services are triggered after the industrial prospect has committed to locate in the area so that the support can be provided at the appropriate time and scale. While supportive facilities and services are necessary for the success of the new branch plant, they represent traditional and passive forms of economic development activity that are needed to support private investment.

There are several economic development project ideas that should be considered when anticipating a new branch plant. First, it may be able to sell products to local firms at lower prices or in greater quantity or with higher quality than currently available. This potential, in turn, may encourage local firms to expand. If potential expansions were not being planned, a venture may be started that purchases inputs from the new branch plant and sells products to local or nonlocal markets.

Second, the new branch plant may want to purchase inputs from local firms, although this possibility is seldom assured, because most branch plants are committed to long-term purchasing contracts or intracompany arrangements. Local firms should be encouraged to market their products with the new firm or initiate a new venture to supply the branch plant with necessary inputs. Commitments from headquarters management should be received before initiating such a venture. If this type of economic development project is to be implemented, management should be advised to begin diversifying the firm's client base as soon as possible so as to reduce the firm's dependency on one customer.

Third, the new branch plant may want to hire employees from the local area. In response a customized training program can be organized to offer well-qualified workers. Local actors initiating this project should seek an informal agreement with the company to give first access to available employment opportunities or a formal "first source" agreement. Depending on the numbers involved, employment increases may initiate a series of multiplier effects in the local economy. Existing local businesses should be encouraged to respond to these opportunities.

If substantial numbers of workers are to be employed at the branch plant, feasible new ventures may be designed to serve the workers, the company, the area economy and the national interest; for example, a limited-service transit venture or an in-plant child care service might be provided. Van service may be feasible to cover the journey to work for most workers, particularly if the plant were run on two or three shifts daily. Similarly, child care service for employees may be provided at reasonable cost. These projects promote area economic development and contribute to the achievement of national goals.

In the event of a *plant closing*, fewer opportunities exist. The anticipated plant closing will free a pool of trained workers and a potentially useful facility. Sometimes firms fail because of local or headquarters mismanagement. In other instances, management intentionally drains profits from the firm without making adequate reinvestments. In still other instances, the firm is simply a losing proposition. Obviously, local actors should determine which facts pertain.

If the firm is viable from an operational perspective, improving marketing and restructuring financing will be necessary, at a minimum, to make the firm a profitable, going concern. Thus an interim or transitional strategy should be devised to identify markets, restructure financing, and improve operations. One possibility is to gain support for retraining workers from the vocational education system or private industry council. For about one year, the firm is turned into a training institution with employee skills development as the primary objective and revenue generation as the secondary objective. By increasing the quality of the work force and maintaining the firm as an ongoing operation, the chances of long-term success are increased greatly once a revised business plan is ready for implementation.

At the same time, local actors have to develop a strategy for purchasing the firm. Employee ownership, community ownership, investor ownership, or some combination of the three immediately come to mind. As noted in Chapter 3, much effort is required to arrive at the minimum purchase price and the most favorable terms of purchase. In negotiating with the present owners of the firm, the advice of corporate acquisition specialists may help strengthen the buyer's position. Getting a good price is important because implementing an innovative ownership and management structure and a sound business plan in a facility for which too much is paid usually spells failure.

As with the new branch plant contingency, timing is important in facing an impending plant closing. Advance notice of a plant closing is extremely helpful but is seldom given. The local development organization should consider requesting first options to purchase facilities from major branch plants in the area. The LDO should ask plant management for sufficient lead time, three to six months at a minimum, to determine the establishment's viability and to make the transitions while maintaining the plant as a going concern.

The potential opportunities in areas suffering from *long-term distress* go beyond the approach of seeking various forms of state or federal support to treat the symptoms of persistent poverty. Local actors should consider the following ideas.

By doing things for themselves, low-income households incur lower labor costs in purchasing consumption goods and services. But because they have little income and no credit, these households must purchase items frequently and in small quantities, thereby increasing costs or forcing the purchase of inferior products. The LDO could survey the consumption patterns of low-income households to identify potential savings from bulk purchases and purchases of high-quality equipment. A purchase-lease cooperative may be minimally profitable if labor were contributed and overhead kept to a minimum. Coop management could purchase products such as fabrics, common auto parts, insulation, and so forth, and equipment such as power tools, sewing machines, chain saws, even a community freezer, at relatively low prices, sell the products or lease the equipment to low-income persons at reasonable prices, and earn a modest profit on the difference.

Considering projects that increase the incomes of limited-resource farmers is worthwhile. One idea is to restructure their product mix so that they produce more profitable crops and livestock. Another idea is to test the local market for less traditional farm products such as herbs, flowers, shrubs, other ornamentals, firewood, and landscaping materials. Cost-saving ideas that are well known to more affluent farmers can be shared with smaller, poorer farmers.

Commercial revitalization efforts often involve *historic preservation* of structures in the older, in-town areas. With building costs and interest rates at high levels, the opportunity costs of downtown clearance are becoming prohibitively high. With federal tax incentives, older structures are being renovated to accommodate a mix of commercial, office, recreational, and cultural activities that increase the economic viability of the entire downtown area.

Local projects that have been completed successfully include improvement of access and aesthetics of existing commercial establishments, conversion of older buildings into larger commercial spaces, creation of commercial malls in abandoned mills, warehouses, and other large structures, and renovation of old train stations, dock facilities, post offices, or other obsolete public buildings. Moreover, the new uses of these spaces need not be limited to commercial or office activities. Space may well be in demand for small-scale manufacturing activities ranging from simple machine processing or fabrication to craft production of all kinds (leather, pottery, ceramics, basketry, weaving, book printing and binding, and the like).

In addition to projects creating physical infrastructure for local business, intermediary business support organizations may be created. A *business information center* represents a modest effort to provide technical assistance to local businesses but is seldom self-supporting even if fees for services are charged. A *small-business center* may be more economically viable. The basic idea is to provide a range of business services common to numerous small businesses more cheaply and efficiently than each could acquire separately. The center houses an office manager/administrative assistant, a few secretaries or typists, and shared office equipment (word processors, telephones, etc.). The center may also purchase goods and services on a shared basis. For example, the center may hire a lawyer, accountant, or engineer more cheaply and provide quality services to each affiliated business. The businesses can be either colocated at the center or spatially dispersed.

Local actors should exercise considerable care in attempting to organize a small-business center. People in business for themselves place a high value on autonomy. The center should support and facilitate the business development of each participant separately and not impose undue constraints or restrictions. Each business should have separate telephone lines, letterhead, files, reports, and so forth, and support the center in proportion to use. These points should be kept in mind while marketing the idea to local businesspersons.

Food production, processing, or distribution, broadly conceived as including fruits, vegetables, livestock, grains, fish, and shellfish, may suggest new ventures. A market survey of the existing food-processing, distribution, and retailing systems should point to any possibilities. Some relevant questions would include: Could more food items of one kind be sold in the local market? Is there an untapped market for different food items? Are any food items largely imported? Could better items be locally produced? What minimum level of sales is required to make an investment worthwhile? With metropolitan tastes spreading to all areas, markets for delicatessen foods, special baked goods, natural foods, and ethnic foods appear to be growing. With more household members in the work force, markets for wholesome, relatively inexpensive food that is precooked or easy to prepare are emerging. Local institutions that purchase large quantities of food are also potential markets.

Energy conservation and development may also support new ventures. Many large utility companies offer inexpensive energy audits and low-interest loans to encourage weatherization, heat pump installation, and other energy-saving investments. Opportunities may exist for energy auditors, installers, or suppliers of basic materials. Some communities are rebuilding low head dams and retrofitting hydroelectric generating equipment to produce electricity more cheaply. Especially in smaller communities and rural areas, wood and coal stoves are a feasible source of additional heat. Local markets may exist for cut wood, coal, stoves, exhaust pipes, chimney pipes, flashing, and noncombustible protective materials.

These project ideas are meant to be neither exhaustive of possibilities nor representative of local endeavors. Rather, the intention is to stimulate the thinking of local actors, particularly LDO directors and their staff. Some model projects are innovative in terms of the guidelines set forth in the previous section; others are not. Hopefully, all represent creative responses to threats and opportunities commonly confronted in local economies.

PROJECT FORMULATION

In project identification, local actors define, describe, and partly justify projects. In project formulation, they redefine and determine the feasibility of project ideas. During the project formulation stage, the decision is made whether or not to complete project planning and implement the project. In general, project formulation involves taking one or more attractive project ideas, shaping and specifying each one more and more precisely, rejecting those that appear to be infeasible, and moving ahead with feasible projects.

Local actors should think of project formulation as an interactive process. On the one hand, the project description must be refined and specified. On the other hand, the project's feasibility must be determined. Rather than describe a project in detail and then determine its feasibility, the project should be redefined as each feasibility study provides insights about how to improve it. Thus feasibility testing begins in the project identification stage and is determined on three related grounds: political, operational, and economic feasibility.

Political Feasibility

Although others participate, the LDO clearly has the lead role in determining political feasibility. Contingency planning or strategic planning at the organizational level and planning at an area-wide level will enable the LDO director to delineate the necessary base of local support required to make projects feasible. Feasibility depends on the degree of political support and the extent of political conflicts surrounding potential projects.

Generally speaking, determining political feasibility is equivalent to evaluating economic development projects and deciding which ones should be carried out. Thus the political element is added to the technical determination of feasibility when key actors agree to commit resources to worthwhile projects.

Benefit-cost analysis, cost-effectiveness analysis, or fiscal impact analysis may be used to determine political feasibility. The economic development checklist may also be applied. By raising a wide range of potentially relevant issues, the checklist can provide a structure for identifying and resolving differences among key actors to gain a consensus on the project. Subsequent feasibility studies are relevant only to projects that are deemed politically feasible.

Operational Feasibility

Operational feasibility begins as soon as key actor(s) assume lead responsibility for the project. They must be given the autonomy to consider alternative operational possibilities and to make choices concerning the specific nature and scale of the project. For a business development project, the operational plan shows which inputs are used to produce the commodity and how the means of production, both material and human, are constructed, assembled, and organized to commence production. Alternative technologies and production arrangements are considered. Operational plans contain estimates of major project costs and schedules for beginning normal operations.

Upon completion of operational plans, the LDO staff should evaluate proposed techniques of production and control and proposed staffing patterns to see how these proposals square with the type of technology, the amount and quality of employment opportunities, the attractiveness of management styles, or other important evaluation criteria considered in the economic development checklist. The operational plans should also be reviewed to see whether the good reputation of the entrepreneurs and their presumed corporate capabilities are reflected in the actual plans developed for the project. These plans become the documents used to initiate the next stage of the project cycle—detailed design.

For a real estate development project, the developer is responsible for the operational plan that addresses site selection and improvements, construction, permits and approvals, interim financing, and other tasks that must be completed to begin leasing (or selling) the space. The size and complexity of the project provide good indicators of whether local or national development firms should be invited to consider the project. In reviewing plans, the LDO staff should be particularly concerned with the developer's capability and reputation, to be reasonably certain that the project will be well executed.

In the rest of this chapter and in the next three chapters, we will consider only economic development projects that (1) are jointly planned and executed by the public and private sectors and (2) jointly fulfill important objectives of both sectors, in other words, public–private partnerships. Business development projects are referred to as public–private ventures. Real estate development projects are called co-development projects.

The justification for having local governments actively engaged in business ventures or co-development is not well articulated. They are simply doing it to realize their growing concern for economic development in the face of fiscal limitations. Yet we must look at these activities closely to determine if they represent a legitimate role of government. The approach followed below is, first, to address the nuts-and-bolts aspects of public–private development projects in considering the issues of market feasibility and financial feasibility, and then to discuss the policy questions in Chapter 9.

Economic Feasibility

Local actors should examine the economic feasibility of public–private projects in several stages. The initial assessment of economic feasibility should be general, considering overall profitability and levels of risk. If the results look promising, more detailed market research, financial analysis, and marketing plans should be developed. Although the entrepreneurs and developers are responsible for the market studies, the LDO staff should help identify additional expertise, such as management or economic development consulting firms, SBA-supported university centers, state or county agricultural extension agencies, or retired businesspersons possibly affiliated with a local Senior Corps of Retired Executives (SCORE) program.

To begin the first-cut market study, the project's output must be precisely described. For a business development project, the commodity is the good or service to be sold in local or nonlocal markets. For a co-development project, the product is space to be leased or sold to business occupants. For both types of projects, it is important to focus on the goods and services that ultimately reach consumers and answer these questions: Which products will be offered for sale? Who are the potential customers for the product? Where are they located? Why would they buy this product? How frequently? It is important to look at market size and trends. Is the product in a growth industry? Is the market area growing or declining? Is the expected size of the market sufficient to begin operations? Estimates of the market should be made in a three- to five-year time frame, both in terms of total units and dollar volume. Next, the competition should be analyzed. What are the strengths and weaknesses of the product relative to the competition? What is the market capture strategy, that is, how will management go about attracting customers? Based on answers to these questions, likely sales estimates and conservative estimates, again in units and dollars, are made.

Entrepreneurs and developers are responsible for the marketing plan. Its main elements are addressed in considering the following questions: How will these sales estimates be achieved? How will initial customers and then additional customers be reached? What aspects of quality, price, and service will be emphasized to generate sales? How will the product be priced? How will the product be promoted or distributed? How will maintenance or servicing be handled? How will the product be advertised? These questions embody the "4 *Ps*" of marketing—product, price, promotion, and place.

Upon answering these questions, entrepreneurs and developers will have two valuable bits of knowledge. First, they will know how to shape and modify the project to enhance its economic feasibility. Second, they will know how to structure the formal marketing plan for project financiers and for the staff expected to take over the project to begin normal operations. Market analysis is addressed more fully in Chapter 8. If the project appears to have an adequate market, its financial feasibility is considered next.

The financial plan contains all of the pertinent dollar estimates that have been made in the other feasibility studies. For business development projects, these estimates are organized in three financial statements—a balance sheet, an income statement, and a cash-flow statement. The balance-sheet format can also be used to develop a sources and uses of funds statement. The income statement contains profit and loss forecasts which are based on estimates of sales and costs. Generally, forecasts are made for at least three years from the year of initial operations. The statements containing estimates and forecasts are called pro forma statements. The cash-flow statements show monthly estimates of inflows and outflows (receipts and payments) for at least the first year of operations. Thereafter quarterly or even annual estimates usually suffice. By revealing the timing of revenues and expenditures, the analysis indicates the amounts of cash needed by the business to sustain normal operations.

Pro forma balance sheets should be provided for the start of normal operations and for the end of the first three years of operations. Unlike the other financial statements which contain estimates of economic flows, the balance sheet lists economic stocks—the assets and the liabilities or promises to pay for these assets. The year-end pro forma balance sheets show the assets used in the operations and, through the listing of liabilities, the financing provided for these assets. The initial balance sheet can be structured as a sources and uses of funds statement listing the type and cost of opening assets and the opening liabilities and equity, which indicate the sources and methods (instruments) of project financing. Thus this statement is

TABLE 7. Financial Statement Formats for Business Development Projects

---

Pro forma income statement (for a hypothetical manufacturing operation)

Sales
  less: discounts and bad debts
  less: materials used
       direct labor
       mfg. overhead (rent, utilities, leased equipment, fringe benefits)
       depreciation
  Total cost of goods sold

equals: Gross profit (or loss)
  less: sales expense
       administrative expense
       expense of management assistance (legal, accounting, etc.)

equals: Operating profit (or loss)
  less: interest to be paid
       taxes to be paid

equals: Net profit (or loss)

Cash-flow statement

Cash balance: opening
  add: cash receipts
      collection of accounts receivable
      misc. receipts (interest received)
      loan proceeds received
      equity investments received
      Total receipts

  less: disbursements for accounts payable
       direct labor
       mfg. overhead
       sales expense
       administrative and other expense
       tax payments
       interest payments on loans
       loan repayments (principal only)
       assets acquired
       Total disbursements

  Cash increase (decrease)

Cash balance: closing

(continued)

TABLE 7 (continued)

Pro forma balance sheet

Assets
  Current assets
    Cash
    Notes held or accounts receivable
    Inventories
    Prepaid items
    Total current assets

  Fixed assets
    Plant and equipment
       less: accumulated depreciation
    Net plant and equipment
  Other assets (identify)

    Total assets

Liabilities and equity
  Current liabilities
    Notes payable to banks
    Accounts payable
    Accrued wages, taxes, expenses
    Total current liabilities

  Long-term loans and notes
  Other liabilities (identify)

  Investor/entrepreneurial/management equity
  Capital surplus/reserve
  Retained earnings

    Total liabilities and equity

Source: Formats for flow statements were adapted from Brian Haslett and Leonard E. Smollen, "Preparing a Business Plan," in *Guide to Venture Capital Sources,* 4th ed. Stanley M. Rubel, ed. (Wellesley Hills, MA: Capital Publishing Corporation, 1977).

TABLE 8. Financial Statement Formats for Real Estate Development Projects

Project development costs

  Site acquisition
  Site improvements
  Construction costs by structure/complex
  Hard development costs

  Architectural and engineering fees
  Permits, bonds, and approvals
  Interim financing
    Closing costs and fees
    Debt service
  Developer's fee
  Contingency
  Soft development costs

    Total Cost of Project
    Cost per square foot

Project income and outlays

  Gross rents or leases
    less: vacancy contingency
  Effective gross rents or leases
    less: advertising
            maintenance and repairs
            utilities
            insurance
            property taxes
            management fees
            other operating expenses
  Net operating income
    less: debt service
  Before-tax cash flow

  Net operating income
    less: interest paid
            depreciation
    Total taxable income
    Tax paid (credit) at applicable rate

  Before-tax cash flow
    less: tax paid or add tax credit
  After-tax cash flow

(continued)

TABLE 8 (continued)

Proceeds from sale of project

Gross sales price
  less: sales commission
           closing costs
           mortgage balance

Before-tax, net proceeds of sale

Original cost of project
  add: improvements
  Cost basis of project
  less: accumulated depreciation
  Book or net value of project

Before-tax, net proceeds of sale
  less: book value of project
  Taxable gain
  less: recapture*
  Long-term taxable gain

Taxes on capital gain
  add: taxes on ordinary income (recapture)
  Total taxes paid

Net proceeds of sale before-tax
  less: total taxes paid
  After-tax proceeds of sale

---

*Recapture is the difference between accelerated depreciation and straight-line depreciation charged over the life of the project. The difference is taxed as ordinary income. Because the entire amount of accelerated depreciation is recaptured as ordinary income in commercial and industrial projects, straight-line depreciation is usually applied to these projects.

Source: Compiled by author.

the basic account that is used to assess different project-financing possibilities.

Considering project risk and reward, the cash-flow statement addresses primarily the issue of risk. The income statement contains information that reveals the potential rewards. The balance sheet is used to assess both risk and reward. Examples of these financial statements are shown in Table 7. (See Rubel 1977.)

For real estate projects, the statements are developed on a cash basis (not on an accrual basis, as is typical for balance sheets, income statements, and sources and uses of funds statements). One statement provides a listing of project assets and their estimated cost, thereby showing the uses of project financing. A flow statement summarizes annual revenues and expenditures. Since real estate often appreciates over time, a third statement is used to show the capital gains (or losses) estimated at the time of the sale. Sample formats for these three statements are given in Table 8.

Project entrepreneurs, developers, LDO directors, and local bankers will be involved in gauging financial feasibility. Each will bring a somewhat different perspective to the analysis. Entrepreneurs and developers will use the financial plan to attract potential investors and to discuss loans with local bankers. Bankers will use their analysis to consider credit risk and other risks inherent in the project. LDO directors will assess the project's financial feasibility in light of public economic development objectives. Furthermore, entrepreneurs or developers often disagree with bankers about the feasibility of a project. In these instances, LDO directors need an independent basis to engage in useful dialogue with the private participants of the project. Therefore, the LDO staff must be able to evaluate market research and financial feasibility studies to have an independent means of judging potential sales, profitability, and risks of the project.

Viewed together, these feasibility studies constitute sections of a typical business plan or real estate prospectus—the market analysis and the marketing, sales, operational and technical, and financial plans. Thus the studies completed for project formulation are also used to market, finance, and execute the project.

The determination of financial feasibility depends on properly structuring the financing of a project and assessing its profitability, liquidity, solvency, and growth potential. These issues are addressed, both for business development projects and real estate development projects, in Chapters 6 and 7, which examine project financing in considerable detail.

NOTES

1. The benefit-cost framework compares the outputs of the project that contribute to aggregate consumption and other *national* benefits against the opportunity costs of resource inputs. The concern is with discounted net social benefits that are defined in welfare (micro)economic terms. On the other hand, most local actors understand economic development in terms of economic base theory, which is couched in a macroeconomic framework. They are primarily concerned with *local* employment and local tax-revenue impacts. Yet labor and tax expenditures are project inputs or costs in benefit-cost terms. They pay little attention to what is produced, but these project outputs represent the benefits in the benefit-cost framework. The tensions between the local and national perspectives are addressed in Chapter 9.

2. The formulas for calculating net present value are given in the notes to Chapter 7, where discounting is used in the case studies and exercises.

3. S corporations, formerly called subchapter S corporations, are companies with 35 or fewer stockholders who receive all corporate profits or losses but still enjoy limited liability protection.

6

FINANCING LOCAL PUBLIC–PRIVATE DEVELOPMENT PROJECTS

Project financing is the most important task in the project cycle after project identification. While the latter determines the ends of local economic development as embodied in a specific project, the former determines the means required to support the project, namely, the sources and methods of project financing. The feasibility studies done as part of the project formulation stage provide estimates of the amount of required financing.

Various financing instruments are needed to initiate business or real estate development projects. Real estate projects and business starts normally require temporary or construction financing, financing to meet organizational expenses, as well as long-term permanent financing. Expansions usually require additional infusions of equity or debt capital above and beyond current levels. Acquisitions and revitalization efforts often call for the revaluation of assets and the restructuring of existing financing to improve the viability of the project.

The sources and uses of funds statement, structured as the anticipated opening balance sheet of the project, should be used to summarize project financing. Uses of funds are the current dollar values of cash, inventories, prepaid expenses, machinery, equipment, facilities, land, improvements, closing costs, organizational expenses, and contingencies needed to start, expand, or acquire a business or execute a real estate project. Sources of funds indicate from whom the financing will come. Owners provide equity financing equal to the initial net worth of the project. Creditors provide debt financing, which establishes the initial liabilities or the external claims on project assets. See Tables 7 and 8.

For any businesss or real estate development project, a wide variety of uses and sources of funds profiles is possible within the context of public–private partnerships. While specific elements depend on the particular project, the structure of project financing depends on two elements, one political and the other technical. The political element is the role that the local public sector has established and agreed to fulfill in economic development. The technical element is the application of development financing principles. (See the glossary of terms at the end of the chapter.[1])

SOURCES OF DEVELOPMENT FINANCING

Traditional development projects involve public investments providing infrastructure or public facilities that support subsequent private investments. As noted in Chapter 4, these projects have been financed from local revenues, government grants, and tax-exempt bonds. Emerging development projects are conceived to be public–private projects promoting business development or real estate development. The relevant sources of economic development financing are different, as emphasized in Figure 6. Sources in the money economy are either direct or indirect. From the direct sources, financings by individuals and business entities are emerging as substitutes for depleted government grants. From the indirect sources, tax-exempt markets do not provide the only source of capital. Other capital markets will also be drawn upon as sources of development funds. In the nonmoney economy, both in-kind contributions and barter transactions will become more important sources of project financing.

In other words, traditional sources of financing for economic development projects are either diminishing or becoming vulnerable to changes in public policy. Government grants are no longer available in sufficient quantity to sustain former activities (let alone meet new needs). Tax-exempt bonds are becoming used so widely that restrictions are being placed on the use of tax-exempt securities. Thus accessing nonmoney sources of financing, directly placing securities with individuals and businesses, and attracting other debt or equity capital from financial intermediaries are becoming increasingly important. The challenge is to justify the proposed uses of funds in

FIG. 6. Traditional and Emerging Sources of Development Finance

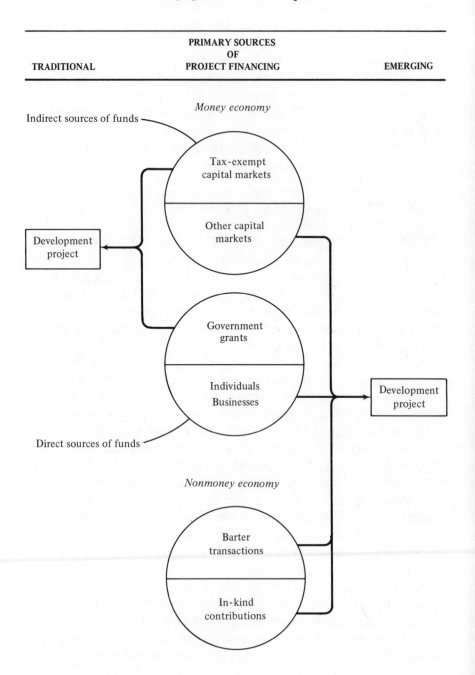

comparison to the public or private alternatives, to secure adequate financing from alternative sources, and to apply these funds to joint public–private development projects that yield adequate social and private returns.

Equity Financing

For the going concern, equity capital generates less risk and secures greater control than an equivalent amount of debt capital, as noted in Chapter 4. For newer businesses and small real estate ventures, equity financing is generally scarce and is a major barrier to economic success. Private participants show their financial commitment to the project by putting up equity capital. In return, they own and exercise control of the venture. Equity capital usually needs to be committed *before* debt capital can be accessed.

When a major corporation initiates an investment project, the equity comes from internal savings (retained earnings), from the sale of securities to investors, typically wealthy individuals, family trusts, finance companies, or insurance companies (private placements or offerings), or from the sale of securities to the public (public placements or offerings). When an experienced businessperson begins a venture, the equity comes from personal savings, a wealthy "backer," or a venture capitalist. A local government can finance its capital investments from accumulated surplus (savings), intergovernmental transfers of funds from state or federal levels, or municipal bonds (either general-obligation or revenue). The accumulated surplus and intergovernmental transfers represent the nondebt portion of the investment, which is similar to equity in the private sector. Which of these sources of equity financing are accessible to public–private projects?

Without an established business record or corporate ties, a new business cannot raise funds from the public placement of securities. Local government surplus funds are not available due to the legal restrictions on the use of such funds. Venture capitalists are not interested because the projects are rarely sufficiently profitable. (On average, venture capitalists are very selective, financing very few of the financing requests that they receive.) Realistically speaking, the potential sources of equity financing are personal savings, government grants, investments of local wealthy persons, or sweat equity.

The entrepreneurs or developers affiliated with the project should be expected to make an equity investment in the project out of personal sources as an indication of commitment to the success of the project. Given the individual's net worth, a balance should be struck between overcommitment and undercommitment of funds. Of course, equity investments by entrepreneurs, developers, and other investors establish private ownership participation in the project and the share of net profits accruing from operations.

Generally, wealthy persons who live in the project area are not interested in investing in local economic development projects since they can maximize returns on their portfolios by making other investments. However, such persons often have a strong personal identification with the locality and may be willing to put some money at risk to help initiate a project that they perceive to be worthwhile. Furthermore, limited partnerships can be used to raise equity for real estate projects or for the fixed assets of business development projects. Limited partnerships can be structured to make the after-tax return on investment competitive for persons in high income tax brackets.

State and federal grants can be used as "near equity" to help capitalize local projects, although the available funds are shrinking. HUD's Community Development Block Grant program, the Urban Development Action Grant program, and SBA's 503 program will probably remain viable sources of funding. However, these sources should be structured as loans to project owners and not as grants.

Local officials should not be mesmerized by the availability of government grants. They should be certain that the community is truly interested in realizing the economic development project. They should prudently utilize government grants to finance needed assets, not create the need for assets simply because they can be financed through available grants.

Unlike the typical private investment that can access debt financing to complete project financing, the typical small business or real estate development project requires additional equity capital before debt can be sought. These business and real estate development projects will compete less favorably for loanable funds than will traditional projects due to higher perceived risks. Compared to funds borrowed in the past, debt capital borrowed in the future will be more expensive (lent at higher rates of interest or for a shorter term) and more uncertain (committed at variable rather than fixed-interest rates). Current trends in capital markets will make local projects harder to finance by conventional means,[2] and equity financing will be all the more important in the future. Innovative methods and atypical sources of equity will be needed and will require *widespread community support*. Many individuals and organizations will be willing to invest their money and time in the project if the organizational phase of the project cycle has been successful.

Equity financing may be sought from the most affected local groups, the prospective customers, suppliers, or users who will benefit directly from the realization of the project. Suppliers may be willing to make modest investments in anticipation of the sales to be generated through project operations. Customers may be willing to pay initiation fees, membership dues, or special assessments to help defray the cost of capital outlays. Users may be interested in making leasehold improvements or advancing funds for escrow deposits and contingency reserves. Local citizens may be interested in buying shares of stock in a local development organization to provide additional equity financing for business or real estate development projects.

In-kind contributions will often make local projects financially feasible that otherwise could not be undertaken. Land, buildings, machinery, equipment, opening inventories, raw materials, and spare parts may be contributed to the project. Alternately, these assets may be created (collected or constructed) with contributed labor, materials, and construction machinery and equipment. In addition, professional services, like the legal, architectural, engineering, accounting, administrative, and planning services required for initiation of the project, may be offered pro bono.

Additional enthusiasm for the project can be stimulated by barter transactions. Indeed, many talented people may be willing to spend time instead of money on the project. The dollar value of such contributions to the project can be estimated, and a share of equity can be allocated to these persons either individually or through the local organizations with which they are affiliated. Although administratively taxing, such barter arrangements should be considered by LDO directors to increase the project's financial feasibility. As an additional benefit, project ownership will be more widely dispersed throughout the community.

Debt Financing

Business and real estate ventures that are launched with no debt financing fall near the extremes of the risk–reward framework. High-reward, moderate-risk ventures may be so attractive as to have more equity financing than needed to begin operations. Here debt financing is considered for strategic reasons, not out of necessity. Toward the other extreme, creditors may be unwilling to offer financing to start the venture because it is too weak. Most local business and real estate development projects fall between these extremes, tending toward the more risky, lower-return extreme. Given this situation, public–private development projects will not be able to attract high proportions of debt capital. In financial parlance, equity will not be highly leveraged.

For relatively safe, secured loans (low-risk investments backed by collateral or other guarantees of repayment), bankers are usually willing to lend from 75 percent to 90 percent of the total investment. For most local economic development projects, bankers should be interested in lending from 50 percent to 70 percent of total project costs, maybe less. This reality again underscores the relative importance of equity capital, either monetary or in-kind, to fund the asset requirements of the project.

While debt capital is scarce, it should be sought vigorously. Regardless of the other pros and cons, debt financing requires considerable discipline to access it successfully. Local actors planning a project have to analyze, design, and present the project proposal carefully to get a loan approved. Like outside experts involved in the project formulation stage, bankers bring an independent perspective to bear on the project. They can offer constructive critical assessments that uncover flaws and improve the project plan. In terms of the project cycle, the banker helps execute a formal project appraisal; the loan officer participates in monitoring the construction phase and the operations phase of the project. Moreover, debt financing provides for some amount of leveraging of equity, thereby increasing return on investment. This point is demonstrated in the next section of the chapter, with the discussion of growth potential. Debt also offers tax benefits because interest payments are a deductible business expense.

For the marginal dollar invested, debt financing offers lower costs and greater control. Costs are lower because debt capital is usually cheaper than equity capital, which is to say that the interest rate on debt is usually lower than the share of earnings to be claimed by the marginal equity investor. Control is greater because debt capital does not dilute ownership.

As for cons, debt financing increases risk and decreases the flexibility needed to secure additional financing. Risk increases because debt, unlike equity, must be serviced at regular intervals and in exact amounts. Insufficient cash to meet debt repayments causes insolvency and threatens foreclosure. Financing flexibility decreases because, all other things being equal, taking a loan or using up a line of credit reduces the ability to access credit in the future.

A final issue relates to the political feasibility of the project. An inferior project may become politically popular. While steps in the project formulation stage guard against this possibility, debt financing from commercial sources provides another line of defense. Local professionals lacking the political influence to veto an inferior project may be able to turn to local bankers, appeal to their prudent banking instincts, and see that the loan application is turned down.

Thus far we have described the creditor as "the banker" offering debt capital. In actuality, various sources of loanable funds are available. Of the federal government sources, the loan guarantees of SBA and FmHA are important to business development projects, while the HUD and FmHA mortgage and mortgage insurance programs are important to real estate projects. At the state level, various forms of business assistance are offered through industrial finance authorities, business development corporations, industrial revenue or development bonds, and general obligation bonds. Special state real estate development vehicles exist, although most focus on single- and multi-family housing. At the local level, commercial banks, mutual savings banks, savings and loan associations, credit unions, community development corporations, local development corporations (either SBA-certified or locally organized) and suppliers offer sources of credit for business development projects. Insurance companies, commercial finance companies, employee stock ownership trusts, private pension funds, mortgage companies, and real estate investment trusts are sources for local real estate development projects.

The most applicable source of funds depends on the intended use of the funds. Local savings and loan associations or credit unions could be approached for real estate mortgages. Potential suppliers could be asked to offer trade credit which could extend to leasing or lease-purchase agreements as well as short-term loans, factoring, or lines of credit. While many forms of debt financing could be discussed with commercial banks, they are most interested in assets that can be very well secured. Rather flexible financing arrangements may be available from local development corporations. Finally, local offices of the major investment companies may offer attractive financing instruments for certain small business or real estate owners.

Sources, uses, and methods of economic development financing are difficult to discuss further in general terms. What is required is the application of these ideas to actual case examples so that the structure of public–private financing and impact of financing provided by the public sector can be appreciated more fully. Specific business and real estate development financings are presented in the next chapter.

FINANCING PRINCIPLES

The basic assumption of joint investing in public–private projects is that some levels of risk and reward are minimally acceptable *from both the public and private points of view*. Because such projects exceed the minimums both for private risk–reward and social risk–reward criteria, they represent legitimate uses of private and public funds. Investing in public–private projects must recognize and incorporate market discipline and social priorities in identifying and evaluating potential uses of funds. Joint business and real estate development projects should create wealth and jobs.

Matching Principle

The *fundamental rule* of financing that is applicable to public–private projects is to match sources of funds with uses of funds. Any asset or profile of assets representing potential uses of funds can be appraised to estimate current market value, expected future worth, and historic or replacement cost. Market value reflects existing supply and demand conditions for the asset. Future worth accounts for the anticipated returns derived from the use of the asset over its projected useful life. Historic cost is the original cost required to bring the asset into productive use. Book value records the historic cost of the asset. Replacement cost measures the present costs incurred to substitute an asset of equal productivity for the existing asset. If depreciation accurately measures physical deterioration and economic obsolescence, depreciated book value will reflect replacement cost. Assuming perfect information, replacement cost, market value, and future worth give the same appraisal for the asset.

Investors and creditors typically lean to conservative estimates of value, return, and economic life, depending on their degree of risk-aversion in relation to expected rewards. Within estimated margins, the amount, security, price, and terms of financing should match the value, risk, return, and life of assets. For a debt instrument, the loan, note, or debenture may be described in terms of its principal amount, whether or how it is secured, effective rate of interest and whether the rate is fixed or variable, term (the period of time between the closing and the time when all principal and interest are to be paid to the creditor), and amortization schedule (what amounts are due to pay out the instrument over its term). Amount, security, rate, term, and amortization are negotiated, taking value, risk, return, longevity, and the temporal distribution of returns into account. Obviously, many combinations are possible to match the financing to the uses of funds. (See Table 9.)

For most business development and real estate development projects, matching sources to uses cannot be achieved without financial participation of the public sector. The comparison between the principal amount of debt capital privately available and the cost of the project may create a gap that cannot be filled by investor equity. The direct loan programs described in Chapter 4 are structured to provide public sources of gap financing to such debtors.

Security is particularly problematic for business starts. Local real estate development projects offer better security than most business development projects because the land and structures developed are general assets with a variety of alternative uses. With either type of joint project, security available to address project risk may be insufficient, even if personal guarantees are forthcoming from the debtor. Loans from public sources that were subordinated to the security interest of private lenders can bring the exposure of creditors within acceptable bounds without requiring excessive personal guarantees.

Similarly, the project's return may be too low, given the current cost of capital. A public loan at a below-market rate of interest can result in a blended rate (the average of the private interest rate and the public interest rate) that lowers the cost of capital sufficiently to make the project feasible.

TABLE 9. Matching Sources and Uses of Funds

Asset attributes	Financing attributes	Loan attributes
Value	Amount	Principal
Risk	Security	Collateral
Return	Price	Interest rate
Longevity	Term	Term
Temporal profile of earnings	Amortization	Repayment schedule

Source: Compiled by author.

Volatile capital markets and deregulation of financial institutions have made lenders reluctant to offer loans at fixed rates of interest. Indeed, the fixed-rate, 30-year mortgage has become a relic of the past. Variable-rate debt instruments shift most of the systematic risk from the lender to the borrower. The public sector can share some of this risk with the borrower by offering a portion of the required debt capital for the project at a fixed rate of interest.

Another matching problem arises when the term of a loan is too short relative to the expected life of a project or asset. In general, borrowers press for terms that are as long as possible, while lenders prefer shorter terms. From the bankers' perspective, shorter terms decrease maturity risk. Such loans increase the project's risk, however, by reducing its profitability and cash flow due to higher periodic interest payments and debt service payments. Again, a public source of funds can help provide longer-term debt. The SBA 503 program expressly serves this purpose in financing fixed assets.

Finally, a mismatch often exists between the project's time profile of earnings and the lender's preferred amortization schedule. Particularly with business starts and real estate projects with high front-end costs, the project may be expected to lose money for some period of time. Thereafter, the project may generate low earnings before becoming more profitable. Clearly, equal periodic debt service payments cannot be met. Indeed a general matching problem exists between banks and other sources of debt capital that have short-term liability structures and business starts and other projects that become profitable in the longer term. This problem gives rise to the need for "patient money" that was discussed in Chapter 4.

An amortization schedule that better fits the time profile of earnings can be designed using a public source of debt capital. In response to cyclical earnings, payments can be timed to fall due during periods when the project expects peak cash flow. For start-up situations, payments can be deferred during the initial period when losses are sustained, paid at interest only when earnings are low, and accelerated in line with increases in earnings as peak profitability is reached.

Thus public participation can achieve better matching of uses of funds to sources of funds for each relevant asset attribute. In conjunction with private debt and equity, public loans can play a pivotal role in business and real estate development financing while neither investing in continually unprofitable projects nor displacing available private capital.

Financial Ratios and Ratio Analysis

While local development organizations are primarily responsible for evaluating economic development projects by taking the social or public perspective, a basic understanding of the private perspective is necessary to participate effectively and creatively in public–private financings. Like the matching principle, other financing principles are applied to fund business starts, expansions, and acquisitions. These principles relate to the private goals or criteria of business development: profitability, degree of risk, liquidity, solvency, and growth potential. Using historical and pro forma financial statements discussed in Chapter 5, potential investors and creditors calculate comparative financial ratios to judge the viability and attractiveness of the business venture.

Profitability, activity, liquidity, and solvency ratios are listed in Appendix E. The norms that are shown should not be applied as rigid standards but as general indicators of satisfactory financial structure. Of course, the norms vary from industry to industry and by size, age, and other characteristics of the business or real estate project under consideration. Deviations from these norms simply indicate the need to seek explanations to determine why differences exist.

Profitability is reflected in the margins between sales or business revenues and business expenses. Profit margins (gross, net, and operating) are measured as a percentage of sales. The most general index of profitability is the rate of return on total investment, measured as operating profit or earnings before interest and taxes divided by the average total value of assets for the period in question, usually one year. Return on equity is another profitability measure—the ratio of net profits to average net worth.

Turnover ratios show how effectively assets are used to generate revenues. One measure is the ratio of sales to total assets (that is, total investment). These three ratios may be related as follows to show that return on investment varies directly with size of profit margin and amount of asset turnover:

Return on investment = Profit margin × Turnover

or

$$\frac{\text{Profit}}{\text{Total assets}} = \frac{\text{Profit}}{\text{Sales}} \times \frac{\text{Sales}}{\text{Total assets}}$$

Degree of risk, although related to the subjective preferences of potential investors, is usually conceptualized and measured in terms of the variability of profits over time and circumstances. Although variation in return can be measured from historical financial information for any business or industry group, anticipated risk to be encountered in the future is more relevant here. Generally, the potential investors subjectively project the level of risk and prepare to meet it by establishing appropriate levels of liquidity, solvency, and security. Obviously the assessments may vary among equity investors and, in particular, between creditors and equity investors.

Liquidity is the capacity of a business to meet financial obligations at minimum and, optimally, to be able to pursue new business opportunities that arise. Cash is generated from operations and from the sale of assets. Generally, assets are ordered in the balance sheet from the most to the least liquid (with the exception of securities, which are liquid assets usually listed as "other assets"). The two most common liquidity ratios are the current ratio and the quick ratio. The current ratio is measured as current assets divided by current liabilities. The higher the ratio, the more liquid is the business. The quick ratio focuses on only the most liquid current assets—cash, marketable securities, and accounts receivable—again divided by total current liabilities.

Solvency ratios, on the other hand, consider longer-term obligations. The most common is the debt-to-equity ratio, which divides total liabilities by net worth. This ratio is also called the leverage ratio because it indicates how much of other people's money (debt capital) is used per dollar of the owner/investor's money (equity capital). A narrower solvency ratio relates only long-term liabilities to net worth. Finally, the debt ratio is the ratio of total liabilities to total assets. Banks and other fixed-asset lenders are very interested in the solvency ratios derived from the business's pro forma balance sheets.

Other ratios that reflect risk and liquidity are used by creditors in judging the creditworthiness of a business. The loan coverage ratio is the principal amount of the loan divided by the value or cost of the asset(s) and is used to indicate how well the asset(s) serves as collateral for the loan. The debt coverage ratio indicates how well the expected income of the business covers debt and other fixed obligations. It may be measured in several ways. On a cash-flow basis, it is the ratio of net cash from operations to debt service obligations. On an income basis, it may be measured as the ratio of earnings, before taxes, to the sum of interest, fixed charges (leases), and other fixed obligations such as sinking fund payments to retire long-term obligations. A simpler measure is after-tax profit divided by long-term debt. Creditors have parameters for these ratios in mind when reviewing financing requests. (See Exercise 11.)

There are no new financing principles specifically relevant to real estate development that do not also apply to business development. Yet real estate development is sufficiently unique to warrant separate treatment of the private perspectives on project financing. Note that real estate and business development projects overlap when land and structures are among the assets involved in business starts, expansions, or acquisitions. As noted, the focus here is on commercial and industrial real estate projects that provide space for businesses. These businesses, in turn, offer permanent employment opportunities and other economic development benefits.

A real estate development project has a unique profile of assets reflecting its unique investment form. The assets are first developed and then sold or leased to final users. Land, structures, utility systems, developer fees, and financing costs represent the uses of funds. The fixed assets are created by site improvements, building construction, and the installation of materials and equipment.

The sources of funds are related to the various roles played by private actors over the real estate project cycle. (See Figure 5.) The developer fulfills the entrepreneurial function. For projects that require additional equity, the limited partners take on the role of investors. As with business development, commercial banks are involved as financiers. Other public and private institutions are involved in real estate financing (for example, mortgage companies, savings and loans, real estate investment trusts, and insurance companies). The developer, investors, and banker are concerned about the project's profitability, liquidity, solvency, and growth potential, and examine these project features to assess potential risks and rewards. Each brings a different perspective to the project. The LDO staff must understand these perspectives in order to play more active and useful roles in co-development projects.

Of the *profitability* ratios, the developer is most concerned about return on equity. Rather than focus on net profit as measured in an income statement, however, the developer studies cash inflows and outflows in projecting net cash flow, usually for one-year periods. This amount divided by invested equity is called the cash-on-cash rate of return.

Investors and bankers are more concerned with return on total investment. Various ratios can be used to indicate total return. On a cash-flow basis, return on investment is given by net cash flow plus debt service payments divided by invested equity and the original principal amount of debt.

Liquidity ratios are not very relevant to real estate development projects. Nonsystematic risk is more clearly related to the capability of the developer and to the adequacy of the temporary financing available during the project period. Besides reputation, the developer carries insurance in the form of performance bonding for the construction phase of the project. Performance bonds reflect the developer's financial strength because the size of the bond is correlated to the working capital of the development company.

Temporary financing provides the necessary working capital for the project. Usually, contingency funds and reserves are built into the financial design of the project to protect against cash short-falls.

On the other hand, *solvency* ratios are quite relevant. The debt–equity ratio indicates the degree of leverage. From the developer and investor perspectives, higher leverage is associated with higher returns on invested equity, all other things being equal. From the lender's perspective, higher leverage indicates higher exposure and greater risk from the project. The perspectives differ in that the former emphasizes the up side or profit potential while the latter emphasizes the down side or loss potential.

As with business development projects, lenders are concerned about the loan coverage ratio—the principal amount of the loan divided by the value or cost of the project. Note that the cost of the project may not equal its appraised value. The relevant debt coverage ratio when the project is examined on a cash-flow basis is the ratio of net operating income to debt service payments. (See Exercise 12.)

The final consideration for business development and real estate development projects is *growth potential*. The growth of a venture is described more fully in Barry, Hopkin, and Baker (1979), pp. 189–192. Equity growth from internal sources (the business operations per se) is limited to net profits less distributions. In a corporation, dividends paid on common or preferred stock constitute the distributions. For partnerships, such distributions are called drawings. For the sole proprietor or family business, the distributions are the portion of income used for consumption purposes.

The equity growth rate may be expressed as follows:

$$\frac{\Delta E}{E} = \frac{P(1 - t)(1 - d)}{E}$$

where E is the equity or net worth; P is the before-tax profits; t is the average tax rate; d is the average rate of distributions; and Δ is the change in E over the time period.

Before-tax profits may be related to the average return on total assets or total investment less the average cost of debt to tie together information from pro forma balance sheets and pro forma income statements. The expression is $P = eA - iD$, where e is the average rate of return on total assets (A), and i is the average interest rate on debt (D) for the time period. Substituting:

$$\frac{\Delta E}{E} = \left[\frac{eA - iD}{E}\right](1 - t)(1 - d)$$

Finally, the influence of leverage on growth may be seen by introducing the leverage ratio:

$$L = \frac{D}{E}$$

and substituting it for debt and equity in the expression, as follows:

$$\frac{\Delta E}{E} = [L(e - i) + e](1 - t)(1 - d)$$

This last expression can be used to examine the influence of return on investment, average interest rate, leverage rate, tax rate, and rate of distributions on growth rate.

Growth potential is very important in real estate projects. Unlike most business assets, it is not uncommon for real estate to appreciate over time. Capital appreciation can be more attractive than operating profitability to real estate investors. Wealthy investors are attracted to real estate partnerships because losses can be written off against income in the short term, and capital gains can be realized in the long term. While current income is taxed up to 50 percent at the margin, long-term capital gains are taxed at no more than 20 percent.

In a typical real estate partnership, the developer, acting as general partner, raises equity by selling participations to limited partners either directly or through brokerage houses. Brokers charge for selling participations. The process of developer working through brokers to sell limited partnerships is called syndication. Although any fixed asset may be financed through a syndication, the experience is primarily with real estate projects. (See Howell 1983.)

The developer, limited partner, and banker have different perspectives on real estate development projects, which highlight the importance of cash flow, tax shelter possibilities, and capital appreciation. Various financial ratios must be measured to understand the positions of these private actors. As noted, equity investors and creditors have a different order of priorities when considering financial ratios. Equity investors concentrate on profitability and growth. They estimate the necessary overall level of capitalization and try to determine the minimum reasonable equity contribution that they should make. Providers of debt capital focus on liquidity and solvency and view profitability and growth as additional indicators of security.

Given the materials covered in this chapter, we are now prepared to consider specific business and real estate development case studies and exercises presented in Chapter 7. For a fuller treatment of financing principles and financial analysis of business development projects and of real estate development projects, refer to the suggested readings on business and real estate development financing in the bibliography.

NOTES

1. Glossary of finance terms:

Amortization. The schedule of debt repayments over time; equal periodic payments of principal and interest, as in a standard mortgage, is referred to as level amortization.

Balloon payment. The final loan payment, significantly larger than preceding ones because the rate of repayments was insufficient to cover all principal and interest over the term of the loan.

Barter transactions. Exchanges between parties where goods, services, and/or assets are traded directly without money.

Bond. A long-term promissory note, usually with a 10- to 20-year term and secured by assets of the issuer.

Bonds, general obligation. A form of debt capital and method of debt financing that is backed by the full faith, credit, and taxing power of a local government.

Bonds, revenue. A bond that is to be repaid from the revenues forthcoming from the project that it is used to finance.

Bonds, industrial development. A general obligation bond that is used to finance a private business or public development infrastructure such as an industrial park.

Bonds, industrial revenue. A revenue bond that is used to construct, expand, or improve a private facility for the purpose of industrial development or pollution control.

Business development corporation. An independent financial intermediary usually funded by a group of commercial banks operating in a state to make loans to businesses that are too risky to receive financing from one bank.

Capital, debt. Financing that establishes an obligation or promise to pay and usually a lien on project assets.

Capital, equity. Financing that establishes the ownership and net worth of a project. *Financial* equity capital is a money investment in the project. *Real* equity capital invests an asset or a service in the project.

Capital, venture. Equity capital usually invested during the planning phase, involving management to increase growth and going-concern value, and aimed at making substantial capital gains within seven years.

Capital goods. Machinery, equipment, or facilities that can be used directly as required assets or can be used to construct or otherwise create project assets.

Capital surplus. The amount paid by investors to the issuer of stock on original issue that is in excess of the par value of the stock; also called paid-in capital.

Capitalization. The amount of total financing needed to start a project or launch a venture, sometimes limited to long-term capital that includes long-term debt, preferred stock, common stock, capital surplus, and, for going concerns, retained earnings.

Collateral. Assets pledged to a lender to secure a loan. If the borrower fails to repay the loan, the lender can liquidate the assets to pay the loan balance.

Contributions, in-kind. Inputs of goods or services, such as labor power, instead of money inputs.

Debenture. A long-term debt obligation usually not backed by any collateral and often convertible to equity.

Debt service. The total amount of principal and interest to be repaid on a loan.

Factoring. The lender or factor advances funds to the borrower in exchange for receivables and/or inventories. The factor makes collections on the receivables and the borrower pays interest on the advances.

First mortgage. A lender's first claim on the proceeds of real estate that may be liquidated through foreclosure.

Lease-purchase agreement. A negotiated agreement to lease an asset over time and make a final payment to assume ownership at some future point in time.

Leveraging, or trading on equity involves borrowing at a lower rate of interest and investing the funds in an asset in order to secure a higher return and more rapid growth on the amount of equity invested.

Lien. A lender's security interest in an asset.

Line of credit. A source and maximum amount of short-term credit that can be borrowed during any one time period.

Loanable funds. The amount of money and credit controlled by financial intermediaries and available for investments at any point in time.

Loan agreement. The legal document binding the lender and borrower to terms of the exchange including amount, rate, term, and amortization of debt; also, description of the specific uses of funds, restrictions/requirements placed on the business (covenants), and procedures to be followed in case of default.

Loan guarantees. A promise to repay any outstanding principal and (usually) interest on a loan made by a third party. When a business borrows funds, the owner often has to offer a *personal* guarantee to repay the loan. Public agencies administer several programs that offer *government* guarantees to lenders providing business loans.

Loans, secured. A loan backed by the borrower's collateral, guarantees, or other promises to repay.

Loans, unsecured. A loan not backed by such assurances.

Maturity. Debt instruments may be short term (less than one year), intermediate (1–7 years), or long term (7–20 or 30 years).

Net worth. The difference between total assets and total liabilities.

Note. A promise to pay principal on demand (demand note) or at a specific point in time (promissory note) and specifying rate and amortization schedule.

Point. One percent, for example, an interest rate 2 points over the prime rate is the prime rate plus 2 percent.

Portfolio. The combination of financial assets held by an individual or legal entity.

Prime rate. The interest rate charged by commercial banks to their most credit-worthy customers for short-term loans.

Pro bono. From *pro bono publico* (for the good of the public).

Puts/calls. Options to sell or buy securities. Most typically, an investor may impose the option to sell (put) shares of stock back to the company within some period of time and at a set price. Alternatively, an issuer of bonds or debentures may impose the option to buy (call) the obligation from the lender within some time and at a set price.

Retained earnings. The accumulated profits and losses of a company less dividends paid.

Return on investment. The revenues accruing to equity owners of the investment; the most common comparative measure of the realized profitability of an investment is the ratio of these revenues to total assets (total investment).

Risk, systematic. The risk inherent in operating a business under prevailing economic conditions that affect all firms.

Risk unsystematic or nonsystematic. Risk specific to a particular firm related to its management, technology, size, cost structure, marketing, industry characteristics, and so forth; lenders are concerned with nonsystematic financial risk, which includes credit risk, collateral risk, and maturity risk. Credit risk is the probability that the loan cannot be repaid; collateral risk is the probability that liquidation value of the security will not cover the principal balance of the loan; and maturity risk is the probability that these financial risks will increase over time.

Second mortgage. A claim on real estate that is subordinated to the claim of the first mortgage.

Sweat equity. The equity ownership accumulated through giving one's unpaid labor to the realization of a project in return for a share of ownership; a barter transaction exchanging labor for a share of the assets created by such effort.

Term loan. Debt capital extended to a borrower for a term of 2–10 years.

Warrant. An option to purchase common stock at a set price and within a set period of time.

2. Banks set interest rates in response to national and international economic conditions, federal monetary and fiscal policy, and government regulation. If inflation or uncertainty about general economic conditions increases, they will charge more for loanable funds. In addition to costing more, capital may become

less available in the future as capital markets grow more competitive on an international scale. Many communities are currently net suppliers of funds, and greater international capital mobility may mean greater local capital scarcity. Furthermore, more competition among potential uses of funds may increase the transaction costs of obtaining financing locally.

7

LOCAL PUBLIC–PRIVATE PROJECT FINANCING: CASE STUDIES

The case studies in this chapter and the related exercises offer an introduction to financing joint economic development projects from private and public sources. The case studies address the financing of each type of public–private development project mentioned in prior chapters: business starts, expansions, and acquisitions, and nonresidential real estate development. The coverage is not meant to suggest that all such types of development projects deserve to be financed. Some communities will choose to restrict eligible financings to business expansions or solid real estate development projects. Others will be comfortable with riskier public–private projects.

The examples assume good reasons exist for making a public commitment to the project, given local objectives and circumstances. In other words, the case study projects are feasible on political and economic grounds. The main issue is how to structure properly the financing from both public and private sources. Economic feasibility, particularly market studies, are examined more thoroughly in the next chapter.

The case studies are fictitious. They represent adaptations, modifications, and combinations of actual joint development projects in which the author has participated.

START-UP FINANCING—DCR, INC.

Mr. Dane decided to incorporate a coffee-processing and wholesaling business after starting the operation on a very small scale as part of his specialty food business. He saw restaurants and hotels with reputations for good cuisine within a 250-mile radius as the potential market. The business would involve purchasing raw beans in bulk, roasting, grinding, and packaging the beans to customer specifications, and delivering the prepared coffee to them.

Mr. Dane owned several small businesses in the food sector and had excellent contacts with hotels and restaurants in the area. He had approached his banker, Ms. Sims, to discuss the idea. She encouraged him to prepare a business plan and financing proposal.

At the same time, Mr. Dane began a preliminary search for a site. He found a location and contacted the local planning department about the zoning in the area. The proposed business required a variance, and the planning director was not optimistic about the chances of getting it.

The planning director asked if he would like to discuss his siting and financing needs with Ms. Rubin, executive director of the local development organization (LDO). Mr. Dane answered affirmatively.

Mr. Dane and Ms. Rubin met shortly thereafter to discuss the new business. Ms. Rubin was impressed with Mr. Dane's business experience and market analysis for the new venture. After reviewing the business plan and financing proposal, she believed that the start-up supported the city's employment and economic objectives and deserved financial consideration. Ms. Rubin indicated that the LDO could offer limited start-up financing as long as sufficient private financing was committed, and the ultimate financing proposal was favorably reviewed by the LDO loan committee.

Within two weeks the LDO received word from Ms. Sims that her bank would be willing to provide Mr. Dane with a line of credit and a term loan to help initiate the venture. However, Mr. Dane did not have a site for the new business or enough money to purchase or renovate a facility. Although most small businesses typically lease real estate, Ms. Rubin suggested the purchase of a vacant building on the fringe of the central business area and adjacent to the poorest neighborhood in the city. Mr. Dane was initially skeptical of the suggestion but soon became convinced that the facility could be purchased at an attractive price and that the nearby labor pool met his needs. Ms. Rubin found the project attractive because it would create five jobs for lower-income individuals and generate tax revenues in excess of the cost of government services.

Mr. Dane prepared a financing package and financial analysis of the proposed venture for LDO review. What follows is a *simplified* version of that work.

Dane Coffee Roasting—Pro Forma Income Statements

	1985	1986	1987	1988	1989
Sales	80,000	110,000	150,000	160,000	160,000
Operating profit	1,000	6,000	11,000	11,500	12,000
Net profit	(1,500)	1,230	4,000	4,200	4,500

Figures are in dollars.

Dane Coffee Roasting—Balance Sheets

	Opening End Year 1984	Pro Forma December 31, 1985
Cash	6,000	900
Inventories	16,000	24,000
Current assets	22,000	25,400
Fixed assets	62,000	62,000
Less: accum. dep.	0	6,700
Net fixed assets	62,000	55,300
Total assets	84,000	80,700
Current liabilities	22,000	25,000
Term loan	24,000	19,200
LDO loan	30,000	30,000
Net worth	8,000	6,500
Total liabilities and net worth	84,000	80,700

Figures are in dollars.

Dane Coffee Roasting—Proposed Sources and Uses of Funds, End Year 1984

Uses

Inventories

Raw materials	10,000
Final goods	6,000
Machinery	15,000
Delivery vehicles	9,000
Real estate	30,000
Improvements	8,000
Contingency reserve	6,000
Total uses	84,000

Sources

Line of credit	22,000
Term loan	24,000
LDO loan	30,000
Equity	8,000
Total sources	84,000

Figures are in dollars.

Proposed Financing for Dane Coffee Roasting, End Year 1984

Line of credit

Amount:	$22,000
Term:	Renegotiated annually
Interest rate:	Four points over prime
Repayment:	Half of the outstanding balance due annually plus quarterly interest on entire balance outstanding
Purchaser:	Commercial bank
Collateral:	Blanket lien on all assets of the business
Use of proceeds:	Inventory build-up and contingency reserve

Term loan

Amount:	$24,000
Term:	Five years
Interest rate:	One point over prime
Repayment:	Level monthly payments of $546 (at 13% interest)
Purchaser:	Same commercial bank
Collateral:	Blanket lien on all business assets
Use of proceeds:	Machinery and equipment purchases

LDO loan

Amount:	$30,000
Term:	Fifteen years
Interest rate:	8% per annum
Repayment:	Monthly payments of $100 for the first year; monthly payments of $287 thereafter; balloon payment due at end of term
Purchaser:	LDO
Collateral:	Second lien on the fixed assets of the business
Use of proceeds:	Real estate purchase

Equity infusion of $8,000 for facility improvements, repairs, and start-up expenses.

A LDO specialist took this information and calculated various financial ratios to gauge the viability of the start-up proposal compared to industry norms. From the public sector perspective, the project would cost $6,000 per job. (Industry norms are given in parentheses where applicable.)

Return on investment (calculated using operating profit in 1987 and *initial* total investment)		=	0.13	
Return on equity (calculated using 1987 net profits and initial equity investment)		=	0.50	
Operating profit	1985	=	0.01	(0.06)
Margins	1986	=	0.05	
	1987	=	0.07	
Turnover	1985	=	0.95	(1.50)
(based on initial	1986	=	1.31	
total investment)	1987	=	1.79	
Current ratio	1985	=	1.02	(2.00)
Quick ratio	1985	=	0.04	(1.00)
Leverage ratio	1985	=	11.42	(3.00)
Long-term debt to equity	1985	=	7.57	(0.80)
Loan coverage, September 1984 (based on LDO loan for real estate)		=	1.00	(0.75)
Debt coverage	1986	=	0.025	(0.20)
(net [after-tax] 1986 profits to 12/31/85 long-term debt)				

After reviewing the analysis, the LDO specialist recommended that Ms. Rubin ask Mr. Dane to double his equity investment at minimum and that the term loan and LDO loan be reduced by $4,000 each. For further analysis of this case study, refer to Exercise 13.

EXPANSION FINANCING–S & C CORPORATION

Mr. Besum founded S & C Corporation five years ago as a custom office furniture manufacturing company. Although the company had become modestly profitable, Mr. Besum saw the need to expand sales volume to achieve greater stability and profitability. He decided to approach growing national financial services companies to determine whether any were interested in custom-designed furniture for their new branch offices. While he pursued these potential accounts, companies sent representatives to visit the plant. Unfortunately, they were not impressed favorably with the size and layout of the facility. They expressed doubts about S & C's ability to deliver an adequate volume of furniture on time. From this feedback, Mr. Besum decided to expand his facility to enlarge his customer base, doubling the building area to 18,000 sq ft, adding several new machines, and totally reorganizing the production process to maximize operating efficiency. He projected significant increases in sales and profit margins as a result of a $300,000 expansion and was anxious to secure the financing.

The expansion required 15 additional workers over the next two years to be paid wages that were 20 percent above the county average for manufacturing jobs. The company had established an excellent on-the-job training program and had experienced low employee turnover.

Mr. Besum requested approval from the county revenue bonding authority for $300,000 in bonds. Although the project met the county guidelines, it was too small to attract any local bank to serve as underwriter. Moreover, most area banks were already holding enough tax-exempt securities in their portfolios. Because the job creation benefits and other social benefits were significant, the county authority referred Mr. Besum to Ms. Rubin, the LDO director.

Mr. Besum explained that he had sought industrial revenue bonds to lower the cost of capital to 75 percent of prime. Compared to the cost of conventional financing at two points over prime, this approach would lower S & C Corp.'s capital costs by five points. Answers to Ms. Rubin's questions also revealed that S & C earnings had been low and volatile over the past three years, the company was highly leveraged, the assets owned and net worth were modest, and Mr. Besum was not in a position to provide additional equity capital for the expansion.

A simplified version of the basic financial information follows:

S & C Corporation—Income Statement

	Actual			Pro Forma	
	1981	1982	1983	1984	1985
Sales	700,000	500,000	700,000	1,000,000	1,200,000
Profits, before taxes	50,000	(35,000)	25,000	80,000	100,000

Figures are dollar amounts.

S & C Corporation—Balance Sheets

	Actual 1983	Pro Forma 1984
Current assets	75,000	100,000
Net plant and equipment	255,000	530,000
Other assets	20,000	20,000
Total assets	350,000	650,000
Current liabilities	50,000	60,000
Long-term loans	240,000	510,000
Net worth	60,000	80,000
Total liabilities and net worth	350,000	650,000

Figures are dollar amounts.

Ms. Rubin computed profitability, liquidity, and solvency ratios. She concluded that the business was marginally profitable, equity was highly leveraged, and little working capital was available.

Mr. Besum contended that if new financing were to cost 10 percent, lowering the average cost of pro forma debt to 11 percent, S & C Corp. could experience steady growth in 1984 and 1985. With the growth formula described in Chapter 6, he determined the growth rate of equity in 1984 and 1985 using the following figures:

$A = $ 650,000

$D = $ 570,000

$E = $ 80,000

$e = $ 0.123 (1984) and 0.154 (1985)

$i = $ 0.11

$t = $ 0.20

$d = $ 0.15

Convinced that the growth potential was significant and would generate at least 15 expansion jobs, Ms. Rubin and Mr. Besum worked out a financial package that did not require additional equity but did require that Mr. Besum offer a personal guarantee for the LDO loan.

Without LDO participation, the bank was willing to commit only $180,000 to the S & C expansion (which gives a loan coverage ratio of 0.60). The funds were offered at two points over prime, or 14 percent. Ms. Rubin knew that the bank would increase its commitment to a loan coverage ratio of 0.75 if an SBA guarantee for 90 percent of the principal amount were secured. She proposed a $75,000 loan to meet the 25 percent down payment requirement. Because the loan was collateralized with a subordinated lien on fixed assets and was offered at a low, fixed-interest rate, SBA decided to extend the guarantee. The combination of the LDO loan and the personal guarantee convinced the bank to offer their loan at 12 percent for the first two years, at one point over prime for the next three years, and at two points over prime for the last five years. The following statement portrays the financial design.

S & C Corporation—Proposed Sources and Uses of Funds, January 1984

Uses		
	Machinery	85,000
	Building addition	215,000
	Total uses	300,000
Sources		
	Commercial bank loan	225,000
	LDO loan	75,000
	Total sources	300,000

Figures are dollar amounts.

Proposed Financing for S & C Corporation, January 1984

Commercial loan

Amount:	$225,000
Term:	10 years
Interest rate:	12% for the first two years, floating at 1% over prime for the next three years, and at 2% over prime for the last five years
Repayment:	Level monthly payments of principal and interest or about $3,230 per month for the first two years
Purchaser:	Commercial bank with 90% SBA guarantee
Collateral:	First lien on all assets of the business; personal guarantee

LDO loan

Amount:	⎫
Term:	⎬ See Exercise 14
Interest rate:	
Repayment:	⎭
Purchaser:	LDO
Collateral:	Subordinated lien on all fixed assets; personal guarantee

For additional analysis of this case, complete Exercise 15.

ACQUISITION FINANCING—DLM CO.

Several years ago a large conglomerate purchased a family-owned electronics manufacturing business. The facility was added to the corporation's electronics division. For the next few years, the facility was very profitable and employed almost 100 workers in two production shifts. But a decline in demand coupled with an ill-conceived marketing strategy eventually made the facility the division's least-profitable operation. Employment declined to about 20. In February 1983, the Board of Directors voted to sell the plant by the end of the calendar year. Several potential buyers were contacted. When no serious offers were forthcoming, the corporation notified the union that it intended to close the plant in six months.

The union's district representative, Mr. Corum, contacted the two top managers at the plant to discuss the news. They had been previously employed by the family-owned business and shared the union's interest in keeping the plant operating. For several weeks they attempted to put together an offer to purchase. Mr. Corum worked through his union's national headquarters. The managers contacted the former owners and several local investors. Unfortunately, none of the parties was able to respond affirmatively and in time. However, through their efforts, $15,000 was raised to help pay for legal and technical assistance required to study the feasibility of the acquisition.

Mr. Corum contacted Ms. Rubin, the LDO director, to discuss possible assistance. Ms. Rubin had been aware of the eroding situation at the plant for the past year and was not surprised to hear the news. Although Ms. Rubin understood the importance of trying to retain employment at the facility, she was also aware of the pitfalls of community or employee buy-outs—the difficulty in determining whether the business is viable, the proper valuation of the business assuming that it could operate profitably, the timing and coordination problems with so many relevant actors, and the difficulty of accessing accurate technical and financial information from existing management.

Ms. Rubin responded as follows. She first contacted an outside consultant for help in determining the potential market and economic value of the facility. Next, she asked the LDO business development specialist to begin working on a preliminary analysis and financial design of the acquisition.

Ms. De Vine, the management consultant, gathered information about the industry from the national trade association and talked with several company presidents who ran similar facilities within the state. With this input, she estimated that the markets for the facility's electronic products were growing and that new management should be able to develop a marketing plan that would result in capturing a sufficient market share to support profitable operations. Ms. Rubin convinced the conglomerate that local interest in purchasing the facility was serious and that financial statements and other information were essential for assessing economic and financial feasibility. As a result, the relevant information was sent to Ms. De Vine. The initial analysis was completed in three weeks. The consultant's basic conclusions were that (1) the local facility could be operated about as profitably as the average firm in the industry (average return on investment was 13 percent), (2) the local facility had suffered from neglect by top division management and could be more profitable under concerned management involved in day-to-day operations, and (3) relief from a large general and administrative burden imposed by corporate headquarters could improve profitability further.

The key financial information was turned over to the LDO specialist as Ms. De Vine focused on valuing the business. What would represent a fair offer price? She estimated the value using the discounted cash-flow approach to arrive at present value estimates of future earnings. However, she was also aware that valuations based on other methods would be required. First, creditors would ask for estimates of asset values, both fair market and liquidation value, before approving any secured loans. Second, employees, local residents, and public officials would understand more readily the valuations if derived by simpler methods. These methods would generate estimates that hopefully were not materially different from the present value estimates. What follows is a *simplified* explanation of the application of these alternative valuation methods.

The electronics division provided a recent balance sheet for the facility:

Cash	2,000
Accounts receivable	350,000
Inventories	700,000
Current assets	1,052,000

Machinery and equipment	550,000
less: accumulated depreciation	200,000
Net machinery and equipment	350,000
Real property	400,000
less: accumulated depreciation on building	250,000
Net real property	150,000
Total assets	1,552,000
Current liabilities	200,000
Net worth	1,352,000
Total liabilities and net worth	1,552,000

Ms. De Vine requested an appraisal from a local commercial and industrial real estate appraiser. The 35,000-sq ft facility and its six-acre site were appraised at $350,000.

Ms. De Vine also purchased the services of a national manufacturers appraisal company from Philadelphia to ascertain the value of machinery and equipment. The appraiser spent three days at the facility compiling information. The report, sent one week later, set the market value at $750,000. Ms. De Vine was initially surprised by the high value of the machinery. As it turned out, the machines had very valuable tooling that was not included in the recorded book values. The appraisals were shared with Ms. Rubin but otherwise kept confidential.

With fair market appraisals, Ms. De Vine set out to determine liquidation value. For how much could the assets be sold at a bankruptcy sale? She thought that the real estate could be sold for at least $250,000, given the inherent value of the land and the fact that the facility could be used minimally as a warehouse. The manufacturers appraisal company allowed that, given the status of the market for used machinery and equipment, about $260,000 would be bid at a forced sale. Finally Ms. De Vine examined the value of inventories, mainly final goods inventory—about 60,000 electrical motors valued on a cost basis of $10 each. She called several national firms that specialized in inventory purchases at liquidation sales. From their comments, she concluded that inventories were worth no more than

10¢–15¢ on the dollar. She summarized the appraisals in the following chart:

	Net book value	Market value	Liquidation value
Inventories	700,000	700,000	70–105,000
Machinery and equipment	350,000	750,000	260,000
Real property (land and buildings)	150,000	350,000	250,000
Total real assets	1,200,000	1,800,000	580–615,000

Ms. De Vine next prepared present value of earnings estimates for the facility based on information received from the trade association, the parent corporation, and comparable operations in the state. As a first-cut, she assumed that (1) under new ownership, the facility would generate $3.0 million in annual sales and $95,000 in after-tax earnings; (2) the facility could generate this level of real earnings for at least 15 more years; and (3) fluctuations in earnings due to business cycles would have no net impact on earnings. Using a reasonable range of discount rates, she calculated the following valuations:

Discount rate	Value of the business
10%	722,570
13%	613,890
16%	529,625

In subsequent analyses, she examined an unequal annual flow of earnings, tried to account for cyclical fluctuations and business risk, ascertained more specific discount rates based on alternative returns to capital, and varied the time period for business operations at the facility. When these analyses were completed, she felt more comfortable with the valuation of $700,000.[1]

The final task involved using three other valuation methods that generated less-accurate results but would be easier for local officials and the public to understand. The price-to-earnings (P/E) ratio for publicly traded small manufacturers in the electronics sector varied widely, but normed at 7 to 8. Using these values, a facility generating $95,000 in earnings would be worth $665,000–$760,000.

The second method focused on the facility's balance sheet. Net book value of fixed assets was $500,000. Depending on market conditions, inventories could be worth $70,000–$600,000. Taking the midpoint ($335,000) and adding fixed assets, $835,000 might be a reasonable offering price for the facility, representing about 60 percent of net worth.

The third method involved finding comparable facilities in the state and discussing values with executives and other experts. Using the relationship between return on investment (earnings-to-assets), operating profit rate (earnings-to-sales), and turnover (sales-to-assets), and assuming the values of 13 percent for return on investment, 3 percent for profit rate, and $3.0 million in sales, the final valuation was calculated. Ms. De Vine submitted her report to Ms. Rubin.

Meanwhile, the LDO specialist had ascertained that a $400,000 line of credit was needed to revive operations at the facility, assuming that the inventory was acquired along with the fixed assets. Writing up the assets to market value gave an opening balance sheet (or uses of funds statement), as follows:

Working capital	400,000
Inventories	700,000
Machinery and equipment	750,000
Real property	350,000
Total assets	2,200,000

Ms. De Vine's report clearly indicated that the appropriate price for inventories was difficult to determine. The LDO specialist suggested that the acquiring entity sell off inventory on consignment for the conglomerate. As long as commissions exceeded selling expense, the new owners could earn something on inventories but remove them from the purchase price.

Ms. Rubin was well aware that as the date for closing the facility approached, the buyer's position improved. However, if the conglomerate got discouraged and closed the facility, key employees, customers, and intangible assets would be lost. Ms. Rubin learned that neither the union nor a local investor group could be organized to make the purchase. The union was willing to lend up to $100,000 to a new entity, but did not want to take an ownership position.

Fortunately, one of the company presidents, Mr. Bergman, contacted earlier by Ms. De Vine, was interested and, in fact, had made some discreet inquiries about the terms of sale. Although he could raise only $30,000 for the acquisition, he was able to locate a national business credit corporation affiliated with a major commercial bank willing to extend a $200,000 line of credit and lend up to 65 percent of the appraised value of fixed assets.

Mr. Bergman offered the conglomerate $480,000 for the facility, excluding inventories. The negotiator for the conglomerate rejected the offer. The next offer was for $900,000, with $800,000 of seller financing at one point below prime. The negotiator rejected this offer also but made a counteroffer: $900,000 with $500,000 in seller financing at 12 percent for five years. The next offer was $700,000 with $300,000 in seller financing. The parties ultimately agreed to a price of $750,000 with $350,000 in seller financing.

Mr. Bergman went back to the business credit corporation and received a ten-year loan for $550,000 secured by fixed assets. He asked the union for a subordinated loan of $50,000 to be used for working capital.

He called the new entity the De Luca Manufacturing Company, the name of the family-owned business that had sold the facility to the conglomerate. The financial structure of the acquisition is shown below:

De Luca Manufacturing Company—Sources and Uses of Funds

Uses	
Working capital	400,000
Fixed assets	750,000
Fees and closing costs	30,000
Total uses	1,180,000

Sources

    Line of credit

    Commercial bank loan

    Seller financing   See Exercise 16

    Subordinated union loan

    Equity infusion

    Total sources   1,180,000

For additional examination of this case, refer to Exercise 17.

REAL ESTATE DEVELOPMENT—NEW CENTER

The downtown merchants had organized a committee under the auspices of the local chamber of commerce to study alternative uses for a vacant site that once housed several retail businesses and warehousing operations. The committee interviewed development company officers around the state and hired one to complete a market study of the site's potential.

The developer, Mr. Rich, proposed an in-town shopping center on the 2½-acre site that would bring new commercial facilities to the downtown area and provide better space for several merchants who were currently occupying inferior locations. The plan was well received. The merchants saw it as a vehicle for better integrating the downtown commercial area and increasing the area's customer draw.

However, a substantial financing problem existed. Relative to the development costs of the project, the project's return on investment would not be competitive at the required level of capitalization to attract sufficient capital. Competitive returns could be earned only if additional capital from a public source were available. Because of this financing problem, the committee referred Mr. Rich to Ms. Rubin, who directed the LDO.

Mr. Rich explained the extent of the financing gap that existed for the project and requested that long-term financing be provided at a fixed rate of interest that was below the current market level. Ms. Rubin replied that she was interested in examining the financing possibilities because downtown revitalization was one of the major goals of the new city administration. She asked to review the financial analyses that Mr. Rich had prepared for the committee and had used to arrive at his conclusions. The following information was provided:

Pro Forma Statements of Operations (in $1,000)

Tenants	Annual for years 1–5
Supermarket	84
Hardware	43
Record store	13
Apparel stores (2)	26
Haircutters (2)	16
Other retailers (3)	39
Gross rental income	221
less: Vacancy allowance	13
Net rental income	208
Owner's expenses:	
Operating expenses	2
Property taxes	2
Insurance	1
Maintenance	2
Management fee	12
Total operating expenses	19
Net operating income	189

Estimated Development Costs (in $1,000)

Uses of funds		Sources of funds	
Site acquisition	169	First mortgage	1,100
Site work	75	Invested equity	252
Site improvements	325		
Construction costs:			1,352
Supermarket (21,000 sq ft)	483		
Other stores (25,000 sq ft)	512		
Permits, surveys	8		
Insurance	6		
Bonds	12		
Architectural and engineering @ 4.5%	75		
Legal and accounting fees	15		
Leasing commissions	56		
Developer's fee and overhead	106		
Financing costs:			
Closing costs	10		
A/E inspection fee	12		
Legal fees	7		
Interim interest on construction loan at 14.5% for one year	80		
Title insurance	9		
Working capital reserve	125		
	2,085		

Analyses of Mortgage and Equity Levels

Mortgage

$$\text{Return on total investment (ROI)} = \frac{\text{Net operating income (NOI)}}{\text{Project's economic value (EV)}}$$

or

EV = NOI/ROI

Let the current long-term interest rate = ROI

EV = 189,000/0.135 = 1,400,000

A loan coverage ratio of 0.75 is used to derive the maximum principal amount. The expected financing terms are as follows:

Principal amount:	1,100,000
Interest rate:	13.5% per annum, fixed for 5 years
Term:	5 years
Debt service:	$12,600 per month or $151,200 per year, based on mortgage payments on a 30-year schedule; $1.081 million in principal due after 60 payments
Security:	First lien on all real estate

Equity

$$\text{Before-tax cash flow (BTCF)} = \text{NOI} - \text{Debt service (D/S)}$$
$$= 189{,}000 - 151{,}200 = 37{,}800$$

Cash-on-cash rate of return (COC) = BTCF/Invested equity (IE)

or

IE = BTCF/COC

With BTCF = 37,800, IE depends on COC expected by the equity investors.

COC:	10%	15%	20%
IE:	378,000	252,000	189,000

If investors accept a rate of return of 15 percent and the bank extends a mortgage of $1,100,000, a financing gap of $733,000 remains.

At this point, the project appeared unable to support additional debt, even if a loan were provided on very favorable terms. Ms. Rubin asked a staff member to review the estimated development costs and touch base with several local realtors and appraisers to get their reaction to the operating income and expense figures. As a result of these consultations, the development cost estimates appeared to be accurate, except that all structures could probably be built for $20.50 per square foot. Also, the working capital reserve could be deleted if the developer assumed responsibility for that amount of cost overruns. Furthermore, the income estimates appeared to be too conservative. More realistic estimates raised the operating income to a level of $210,000 per year.

The LDO staff consolidated these figures to revise the calculations of debt and equity levels. Estimated development costs now totaled $1,908,000. Annual net operating income was $210,000. The maximum principal balance was about $1,170,000. The equity investors required a net cash flow of $37,800 annually to offer a $252,000 cash infusion. If a LDO loan were used to close the remaining financing gap, it could not be repaid. (See Exercise 18.)

The project was not financially feasible on a before-tax basis. However, Ms. Rubin knew that more equity could be raised from local investors if they were shown an attractive after-tax cash-on-cash return that included income tax deductions from depreciation expenses and interest payments as well as capital gains from the sale of appreciated real estate. She and Mr. Rich worked together to extend the real estate analysis. Their results are presented below.

Let economic value (EV) = 1,908,000 and net operating income (NOI) = 210,000. Then cash return on investment (COC) = 11.0%.

With a loan coverage ratio of 0.75, the maximum total debt is 0.75 × 1,908,000 = 1,431,000, and the required equity = 477,000.

Assume that a bank were willing to extend a first mortgage loan for 1,100,000 after analyzing the project. A subordinated 30-year LDO loan of 331,000 could be offered to provide the remaining debt financing.

Because the project's overall cash return is only 11 percent and the bank requires an interest rate of 13.5 percent, the LDO loan's interest rate could be set to yield a blended rate of 11 percent. The blended rate is simply the weighted average of the two interest rates, given level payments and equal term for the two loans: $(1100/1431)$ × 13.5 + $(331/1431)$ × i = 11.0.[2] See Exercise 19.

The required equity investment is $477,000. Assuming that the real estate is sold after ten years of operations, net operating income and the cost of capital remain constant over this period, and *the investors have sufficient income from other sources to absorb all of the tax benefits*, what after-tax cash return is possible?

Approach: Find the present value of all sources of cash, which include before-tax cash flow from operations (BTCF), tax benefits (TB) from interest payments (IP) and depreciation expenses (DE) and after-tax capital gains (ATCG) from the sale of the property in the eleventh year:[3]

$$BTCF = NOI - D/S = 210,000 - 167,300 = 42,700$$

Using average annual interest payments (actual mortgage interest payments would *increase* the tax benefits), total interest paid in the first ten years is

First mortgage	=	1,454,819
LDO loan	=	79,828

and average annual interest is set at 145,480 and 7,980, respectively. Thus,

$$IP = 153,460$$

From the figures on estimated development costs, only land (site acquisition and site work) cannot be depreciated. Construction and site improvements can be depreciated on a 15-year schedule, leasing commissions can be expensed in one year, and all other costs can be written off over five years. Using straight-line depreciation, total depreciable costs are 1,268,000, 56,000, and 584,000, respectively.

Depreciation expenses:

Year 1:	56,000 + 116,800 + 84,500 = 257,300
Years 2–5:	116,800 + 84,500 = 201,300
Years 6–10:	84,500

Clearly, tax deductions exceed NOI. The investors would sustain an income tax loss on the project. Because these losses could be charged against other income, the value of the losses depends on the marginal income tax rate paid by the investors. Assuming a 45 percent tax rate and using the formula shown below, the results for the three periods are 90,340, 65,140, and 12,580.

$$TB = \text{Tax rate} \times (DE + IP - NOI)$$

Finally, assume that the net proceeds from a sale in the eleventh year are $300,000. As a long-term capital gain, only 40 percent of this amount is taxable. At an income tax rate of 45 percent, 18 percent of the net proceeds would be paid in taxes and 82 percent would be added to after-tax cash flow. (See Exercise 20.)

$$ATCG = 0.82 \times 300,000 = 246,000$$

Total after-tax cash flow (ATCF) is found by calculating the present value of cash from all three sources. In addition, the equity investment of $477,000 may be introduced as the initial capital outlay required to realize ATCF over time.[4] The task is to calculate *net* present value at various discount rates. In doing the analysis, –477,000 represents the cost sustained in the first period, the combination of TB and BTCF calculated above are applied to the next ten periods, and ATCG is realized in the final period. Net present value (NPV) estimates are given at three discount rates, as follows:

Discount rate	NPV
10%	155,496
15%	44,709
20%	-28,287

In other words, investors seeking a 15 percent rate of return earn $44,709 more than the cash flow required just to compensate them for the initial investment plus 15 percent return. The internal rate of return for this cash flow is the rate that equates initial investment to subsequent cash flow. At this discount rate, NPV = 0. The internal rate of return on this cash flow is 17.8 percent.

Based on this analysis, Mr. Rich and Ms. Rubin determined that the project was feasible, because the after-tax returns were attractive, even considering the higher level of invested equity and the project's inherent risk. New Center became the hub of revitalization efforts that continued for many years.

REAL ESTATE/BUSINESS DEVELOPMENT
FINANCING—JMS GROCERY

(The final case study is examined both as a real estate development project and as a business development project.)

Ms. James had been general manager of an independent grocery for two years since receiving her MBA. She was managing the family business that had been in operation in this small city for over 50 years. She had tried to meet the competition from two new supermarkets that had opened in shopping centers on the outskirts of town but had not been able to sustain sales levels over the previous 12 months. She became convinced that survival required a new business plan. To compete with the grocery chains successfully required: a new facility with adequate and convenient parking; competitively priced products; an attractive interior layout of the store; specialty food centers including a deli, a bakery, a fresh fish market, and a natural foods center; and more active merchandising and advertising of products.

Because she served on the LDO board, Ms. James knew that the LDO supported projects that increased investment in the downtown business area. In addition, her family owned a vacant, 1¼-acre site near the existing store that was an excellent in-town location for the new facility.

She decided to act as developer and general contractor to build the new store. She could make use of her many excellent contacts among local construction contractors and city agency personnel to develop the site. Her business would lease the facility upon completion of construction. She would purchase new equipment and inventory for the new store and move some existing equipment and inventory from the present location.

As developer, Ms. James had to compare the square-foot price of leased commercial space in the downtown area to the costs of developing the site. As business owner, she had to project weekly sales volume and analyze sales, variable costs, and fixed costs to determine the viability of the project.

As a first step, she completed a market feasibility study for the new supermarket. The cooperative from which she purchased store-brand products provided marketing assistance at a reasonable cost. Based on this information, she estimated that the market within 8 miles of the in-town location was over $300,000 per week in expenditures for food items. Currently, her store and the two chains were capturing about 50 percent of this market. However, the chains were generating average sales of almost $5.00 per square foot while her store had average sales of only $3.30 per square foot. As part of the marketing plan, sales in a larger 15,000-square foot facility were to be increased to $3.66 per square foot or $55,000 in weekly sales. The increase was to come primarily from capturing a larger share of the total market and secondarily from the market share currently enjoyed by the local competition.

Based on the assumption that sales could be increased from $3.66 per square foot to $4.45 per square foot in five years, Ms. James assembled the following pro forma income and cash flow summary:

Projected Income Summary (in $1,000)

	Year 1	Year 2	Year 3	Year 4	Year 5
Revenues	2,860	3,003	3,153	3,311	3,476
Labor cost	266	266	266	266	266
Facility lease	90	90	90	90	90
Depreciation	40	67	67	67	67
Interest expense	62	59	54	48	38
Other direct expenses	2,343	2,456	2,575	2,700	2,830
General and administrative	72	72	72	72	72
Net profit	-13	-7	29	68	113

Projected Cash Flow Summary (in $1,000)

	Year 1	Year 2	Year 3	Year 4	Year 5
Net Profit	-13	-7	29	68	113
Add: Depreciation	40	67	67	67	67
Interest expense	62	59	54	48	38
Funds from operations	89	119	150	183	218
less: Debt service	80	78	75	73	73
Cash flow	9	41	75	110	145

The difficulties of the past year had not had a major impact on the business balance sheet. Ms. James expected to end the year with a current ratio of about 2.5:1 and a debt-equity ratio of less than 1.1. Stockholder equity would be about $70,000.

From the business perspective the project seemed feasible. The inventory financing would come from the food cooperative that sold standard-brand products to the store. The equipment financing would come from the national company that would supply most of the new equipment. The required down payments would come out of retained earnings.

The next analysis focused on the feasibility of the real estate development project. The estimated project costs were $630,000. Of this amount, the developer owned the site that was worth $100,000. The developer hoped to finance the remaining cost of the project at 14 percent for 25 years. The business could afford to pay the current rental cost of downtown commercial space—$6.00 per square foot per year. The following annual projections reveal the annual cash flow situation:

Pro Forma Statement of Operations

Gross lease payments	90,000	Supermarket 15,000 sq ft @ $6 per sq ft
less: vacancy	0	
Effective rent	90,000	

less: taxes	5,000	
insurance	4,500	
other operating expenses	4,500	Repairs, maintenance, etc.
Net operating income	76,000	
less: debt service	77,100	25-year, 14% mortgage for $530,000
Before-tax cash flow	-1,100	

The real estate project would become feasible if rents were to increase, say, to $7 per sq ft. While improving the real estate project, this additional $15,000 annual payment obviously decreased the viability of the grocery business.

Ms. James visited Ms. Rubin to discuss the possibility of LDO involvement. Ms. Rubin first determined the political feasibility of the project. In addition to the contribution to downtown revitalization, the project would generate 15 new jobs, seven full time and eight half time. Most of these positions could be filled by the younger members of the low-income families that lived within walking distance of the site. The market and feasibility studies and the operational plan appeared to be reasonable and competently done. Therefore, she concentrated her efforts on generating financing alternatives.

The financing from the coop and equipment supplier appeared secure on the business development side of the project. The mortgage financing was clearly the problem. The real estate project generated only a 12 percent capitalization rate, but the cost of capital was 14 percent. Furthermore, the loan coverage ratio was high, about 84 percent. Clearly, additional equity or near-equity was needed to carry out the project.

Ms. Rubin calculated that the LDO could contribute no more than $55,000 to the project, given the number and type of jobs in question. Being familiar with lending practices of the local commercial banks, she thought accessing more than $400,000 as a first mortgage loan would be difficult. That amount could be increased if the bank were able to secure an 80 percent loan guarantee from a federal agency.

Ms. James allowed that additional equity might be raised if she syndicated the project. Participations purchased by limited partners could raise $50,000 or more, depending on how the offering were structured.

The two agreed to explore these possibilities further. Ms. Rubin discussed the project with other members of the LDO board. They thought that the LDO could offer a $50,000 loan if the project could be shown to be financially feasible. Ms. James worked out the following analysis assuming that one of the local banks was willing to offer a first mortgage loan of $410,000.

To raise the additional equity, Ms. James first established a legal entity to act as project developer and general partner. Participations in the project were to be sold to passive investors whose financial liability was limited to their investment and personal guarantees. She planned to design the partnership agreement so that, initially, 99 percent of the losses were assigned to the limited partners with 1 percent going to the general partner; then 90 percent of the profits were allocated to the limited partners until they had received sufficient return on investment; all residual profits and capital gains realized thereafter were assigned to the general partner. The sources and uses of funds statement outlines the structure of the financing.

JMS Development Project (in $1,000)

Uses of funds		Sources of funds	
Site acquisition	100	First mortgage	410
Construction of supermarket	375	LDO note	50
Other improvements	65	Equity	170
Developer's costs	90		630
	630		

Ms. James had to make several assumptions to compute the after-tax value of the project. First, the first mortgage is amortized at 14 percent over a 25-year term. The LDO note falls due in ten years and requires annual interest payments of $3,000. Second, the supermarket could be depreciated on a 15-year schedule, with other improvements on a five-year schedule. Third, a net operating income of $76,000 is assumed to remain constant over time. Fourth, the investors are in a 50 percent income tax bracket, with sufficient outside income to absorb tax losses from this project.

Income Statement

Year	NOI	Depreciation	Interest	Net profit	Tax benefits
1	76,000	56,000	60,400	-40,400	20,200
2	76,000	56,000	60,084	-40,084	20,042
3	76,000	56,000	59,725	-39,725	19,863
4	76,000	56,000	59,314	-39,314	19,657
5	76,000	56,000	58,847	-38,847	19,424
6	76,000	25,000	58,314	-7,314	3,657
7	76,000	25,000	57,706	-6,706	3,353
8	76,000	25,000	57,013	-6,013	3,007
9	76,000	25,000	56,224	-5,224	2,612
10	76,000	25,000	55,323	-4,323	2,162

The present value of 99 percent of the tax benefits is shown below for each of three different discount rates over the first ten years:

Discount rate	PV
15%	71,700
20%	63,200
25%	56,300

In addition to these tax benefits, the investors would receive the annual, before-tax cash flow of $13,350.

Based on this analysis, Ms. James offered seven limited partnerships for $10,000 each. She described this analysis in a brief "prospectus" and circulated it among local investors. As the prospectus read, the investors received 99 percent of the tax benefits for the first five years of operations and 85 percent of the benefits for the next five years, after a 12-month construction period. The limited partners would earn more than 35 percent on their investments, receiving most of the tax benefits in the first five years.

She sold the seven participations in the form of options rather quickly. Although most of the tax benefits were to accrue to investors for the ten-year period, the development company became sole owner of the property afterwards. In combination with the land contributed by her family, Ms. James now had the required equity and could turn attention to securing a bank commitment for the first mortgage loan.

Ms. James approached her banker, Mr. Rose, with the business plan and the real estate development plan. They discussed the project in considerable detail. Mr. Rose had two basic concerns. First, the cash flow for the real estate project was entirely dependent on rent paid by the grocery business. What if the independent grocer were unable to compete with the chains? Was there a contingency plan for this possibility? Second, the market feasibility study for the grocery appeared overly optimistic compared to figures that he had seen for independents in nearby communities. Based on these comparables, he did not believe that the new facility could sustain $55,000 in weekly sales.

Ms. James allowed she had no contingency plan but argued that the bank would have adequate security given the risk. The first lien on the real estate would comfortably exceed the principal balance of the loan. Moreover, the cushion would increase over time. As for the market feasibility study, she defended the analysis, noting that the estimates were on the conservative side. Although independent grocers in the area were selling less than the chains on a per-square-foot basis, an independent could compete successfully if armed with the type of business plan that she had put together for her business. She asked him what additional information was needed to address his concerns and satisfy the loan committee.

The banker replied that he would discuss the project with the committee within the week. After meeting with the loan committee, he told Ms. James that personal guarantees would be required to allay the concerns of the committee and receive approval of the loan request. The limited partners agreed to sign for the loan. Mr. Rose thought that personal guarantees would be sufficient to satisfy the loan committee.

The loan was approved two weeks later, and site work began shortly thereafter.

NOTES

1. Operationally, discounting is a method used to value at the *same* point in time economic stocks and flows that are created or realized at *different* points in time. Conceptually, discounting is based on the idea that $1.00 worth of consumption today is not equal to $1.00 worth of consumption one year from today. Since most people value present consumption more than future consumption, there is generally a positive rate of time preference.

To find the present value of a uniform flow of future earnings, we use the formula:

$$V_0 = Y[1 - (1 + r)^{-t}]/r$$

where V_0 is the present value; Y is the equal flow of earnings for t time periods; and r is the discount rate reflecting time preference. For example, the present value of $95,000 earned annually for 15 years and discounted at an annual rate of 13 percent is $613,890. Obviously, the present value is much less than the arithmetic sum of earnings—$1,425,000 due to positive time preference.

In addition to time preference, the discount rate can also be chosen to reflect the degree of risk involved in realizing earnings and the returns available from alternative investments.

For any single period, present value can be shown as the inverse of future value. The computation involves compounding rather than discounting:

$$V_t = V_0(1 + r)^t$$

The future value of $100 ($V_0$) compounded annually at a rate of 10 percent (r) for ten years (t) is $259.40.

$$V_0 = V_t(1 + r)^{-t}$$

The present value of $259.40 ($V_t$) realized in ten years and discounted at a rate of 10 percent is $100.

The most basic discounting formula equates the present value of a *perpetual* flow of earnings to

$$V_0 = Y/r$$

For example, if we believed that a company always remained competitive and continually maintained its base of productive assets, then its value as a going concern is its net earnings divided by the appropriate discount rate. With Y equal to $95,000 and r equal to 10 percent, V_0 is $950,000. Note that this value is larger than the one given in the text ($722,570). It can be proven mathematically that the perpetual flow equation is the limit of the discounting equation for a uniform series of payments as time (t) tends to infinity. Notice also that the previous equation can be expressed as

$$r = Y/V_0$$

This earnings-to-value ratio is usually referred to as the capitalization ratio and is essentially the same as the ratio shown in Appendix E. The capitalization rate is the reciprocal of the price (value)-to-earnings ratio.

2. The LDO loan rate is 2.7 percent.

3. The results would change slightly if periods shorter than one year were used in the analysis (for example, months). Also, cash flow is assumed to become available at the end of each period.

4. In a more complete investment analysis, annual estimates of return on equity are calculated. In these return-on-equity calculations, annual principal payments can be added to initial equity to find current invested equity, which can be used as the denominator of the equation. In this case study principal payments of almost $140,000 are made over ten years.

8

ECONOMIC FEASIBILITY
OF LOCAL PUBLIC–PRIVATE
DEVELOPMENT PROJECTS

Sound project planning requires careful feasibility studies to insure that identified projects can be successfully carried out. A *politically feasible* project is one that meets public economic development objectives. (For example, see the Economic Development Checklist in Table 6.) An *operationally feasible* project is one that is workable, physically manageable, and uses appropriate technology. An *economically feasible* project is one that satisfies private objectives pertaining to risk and reward. The degree of private enthusiasm for a project will depend on its economic feasibility. That enthusiasm, in turn, will influence the amount of private resources committed to the project.

The general treatment of project financing in Chapter 6 and the case studies presented in Chapter 7 assumed that the projects under consideration were economically feasible prior to the structuring of financing terms or that they could be made economically feasible with appropriate financing arrangements. In this chapter, we discuss economic feasibility more systematically and thoroughly. In doing so, we assume that the projects meet local development objectives (political feasibility), are technically sound and workable (operational feasibility), and can be properly financed from private and public sources *if* found to be economically feasible.

The determination of economic feasibility requires addressing two sets of questions. One set focuses on the project's potential markets. The other set deals with the project's costs and the relevant investment criteria. Market studies investigate supply–demand relationships and the prospects for capturing an adequate market share. Financial feasibility analysis inquires into potential return on invested capital given projected revenues and costs. Economic feasibility, then, consists of market studies and financial feasibility analysis, or, more concisely, of market and feasibility analysis.

From the range of local economic development projects, the focus here is on local public–private development projects. Consistent with the previous chapter, only business development and real estate development projects that promise increased jobs and tax base and require significant public-sector participation will be considered. The projects include commercial and industrial real estate development projects and small-business starts, expansions, and acquisitions.

Market and feasibility analysis is more explicit and clearly established as a phase of the real estate project cycle. It is treated less explicitly in small business development where it is subsumed as part of the business planning process. The subsequent sections present real estate development first and then consider business development.

REAL ESTATE PROJECTS

In general real estate projects begin with a site or with a specific project idea. If the process of project planning described in Chapter 5 is followed, the identified project will usually specify a site and a use. The essential features of economic feasibility analysis are the same in both instances. Usually, a preliminary feasibility analysis is undertaken first to determine whether a more detailed analysis is required.

The essence of the market study can be described in many ways. The following sequence of tasks attempts to capture that essence. It is more an art than a science. The tasks describe an investigation that should lead to an informed decision about whether to proceed with the project.

- Initial description of the use(s) of the space created by project
- Identification of the market or trade area of the proposed use(s) of the project site
- Analysis of regional and area-wide growth dynamics, patterns, and trends

- Examination of industry-specific conditions and trends which directly bear upon the proposed use(s) of space
  - Site and use-specific analysis of demand
  - Site and use-specific analysis of supply—the project's competition/comparables
  - Development of a market capture strategy
  - Final description of the use(s) of project space
  - Estimated sales or rental value of the space

The feasibility study begins with revenue figures derived from the market study and includes the following tasks:

- Development of pro forma operating statements
- Development of estimated "hard" and "soft" project development costs
- Estimation of before-tax, after-tax cash flow and property appreciation potential
- Analysis of return on investment
- Consideration of project restructuring to increase flexibility
- Decision about the project's attractiveness relative to other uses of capital

Operating statements compare projected revenues with operating expenses, maintenance costs, and debt service. These pro formas are projected for at least three years and, more typically, for five to fifteen years. The statements give estimates of before-tax cash flow.

With estimates of development costs and recognition of the special features of the project (for example, whether a historical structure is involved), estimates of after-tax cash flow and the appreciation potential of the property are made. Using discounted cash-flow analysis, various return-on-investment measures are calculated and evaluated for the project.

For public–private projects, restructuring may be necessary to increase the private returns from the project. The financing arrangements described in Chapters 6 and 7 can be used to improve project feasibility. Ultimately, both public and private actors must decide whether the project represents an attractive application of scarce capital relative to alternative public and private investment possibilities.

The reader will notice that financial feasibility analysis involves the same accounts and considerations that were addressed in the examination of project financing. Therefore, this aspect of economic feasibility need not be analyzed further in general terms. After market studies are described in greater detail, several examples will be given that integrate market information and financial feasibility analysis. These examples will clarify the links that exist between market studies, financial feasibility analysis, and project financing.

The initial description of proposed uses in the market study usually identifies the space as residential, commercial, industrial, or public. Commercial space may be devoted to uses like retailing, offices, and hotels. Industrial space accommodates manufacturing, distribution, trucking, and warehousing. Often projects provide for mixed uses. In this chapter, relatively simple retail, office, and industrial projects will be analyzed for illustrative purposes.

Each category of space has a market or trade area. Population-serving activities produce at a particular location and sell to consumers residing in the surrounding geographic area. Population-oriented activities can be arranged in a hierarchy from the most ubiquitous, serving the deepest consumer markets, to the most specialized. Ubiquitous activities such as service stations or grocers sell in small geographic areas. Specialized activities, like medical specialists, serve much larger spatial markets. Business-serving activities also produce at one location but sell to fewer, more dispersed customers. Business-oriented activities can have local, regional, national, or international clients. Those that sell nonlocally comprise the locality's export base. The growth potential of the export base, although difficult to determine, represents one of the most fundamental economic development questions faced by local development organizations.

The fundamental concept relating to market or trade area is the range of the commodity produced at the site. Location theory and central place theory, in particular, give a conception of profit-maximizing behavior in a spatial context. Techniques for defining trade areas are described in Reilly (1931), Nelson (1958), Huff (1964), and Applebaum (1966).

A broader view of the project is attained by analyzing regional and area-wide growth dynamics. In fact, a common error made in doing market studies is initiating a site-specific analysis without having a more general understanding of local and regional trends. The analytical techniques of economic base, shift–share, input–output, and econometrics can be used to estimate the area-wide demographic and economic trends. Although the economic base model is most frequently applied, other approaches are justifiable. An approach grounded by a theory of economic development is much richer than one that proceeds on a purely descriptive level. Thus we see that the theoretical and strategic considerations raised in Chapters 2 and 3 are very helpful in doing well-informed market studies.

Another aspect of the market study frequently overlooked is the analysis of the industry under consideration. This task is often unnecessary when the developer is experienced and has a firm grasp of industry trends. On the other hand, the local actors representing the public sector are less likely to have experience in nonresidential real estate development. They are well advised to consult experts in retailing, personal and business services, and particular manufacturing specializations to learn about relevant industry trends. Useful information can be found in publications from the U.S. Department of Commerce and from national trade associations. Experts in the ranks of active or retired local businesspersons may also be helpful.[1]

With relevant area-wide and industry-specific growth dynamics firmly in mind, the site-specific analysis begins. A host of factors indirectly affect site use. Access, lot characteristics, zoning, local preferences, external impacts, and parking are among the most important. These factors will circumscribe, if not precisely identify, the potential use(s) of the site.

Demand indicators depend on the use under consideration. For retail space, projections of population, households, and income are most germane. These projections are also needed for projects providing space for other population-serving activities such as personal services and local banking. Office space is a hybrid in that some uses support activities directed at persons and other uses support business-serving activities. One commonly used approach is making demand for office space a function of employment projected for office-using industries, namely finance, insurance, real estate (called "FIRE"), government, and services. Even though these projections are fairly crude, they do offer useful information about overall trends. For manufacturing and other export-oriented activities, space requirements depend on employment projections, which are shaped by the understanding of the broader economic development process as noted above.

Whichever demand indicators are used, the projections must be transformed into estimates of space requirements. Development handbooks report rules of thumb for making these conversions (for example, 200–250 sq ft per office employee). However, local information on space utilization may help you arrive at more accurate estimates of space consumption. Local information may reveal emerging behavioral patterns that are not yet reflected in national norms. For example, firms occupying existing office space may be planning to use the space more flexibly and creatively. Office employees may be spending more time working at home. Both changes would tend to lower the amount of space required per employee.

Demand forecasts for the next five or ten years are compared to the supply of space. Planned and approved projects must be treated as part of the future supply along with existing developments. In a stable or declining situation, potential for new projects is limited, but interest in adaptive re-use or demand generated by the attrition of existing capacity may be great. In growing markets, additional space will be required and mainly derived from new development projects. Vacancies and conversion possibilities of existing structures should also be considered when analyzing sources of supply. Particularly for public–private real estate projects, local development organizations must avoid using their resources to compete against existing business constituents. Effective project organization is one safeguard against this contingency. However, careful supply analysis can also help. Accurate supply–demand forecasts are useful. With better forecasts, all interested developers can improve their projections and plans, possibly modifying the oversupply–undersupply pattern that often plagues the real estate industry.

Developing a market capture strategy is a critical step in the market study. It leads to a final description of the space to be developed and firmer estimates of sales and rental levels. Timing is very important. Regardless of their overall accuracy, supply and demand forecasts must be phased over time to give a clear picture of when space will be needed. The larger and more ambitious the project, the longer is the time frame, and the greater is the uncertainty. The strategy also depends on the type of space being provided. When little uncertainty and deep markets are present, projecting net demand, establishing fair-market sales or rental levels, determining financial feasibility, and moving directly to construction financing may be sufficient. A project creating retail space for convenience goods stores in a rapidly growing section of the city serves as an example of this type of project. For most projects, however, more detailed planning will be necessary.

An effective market capture strategy depends on the resources and talents of the developer. Additional research on the tastes and requirements of space users is often helpful. Prospective tenants can be surveyed. Comparable properties identified while making supply estimates can be visited. From this analysis the project's capture rate is estimated.

At this stage negotiations with investors and lenders begin. Rarely are developers encouraged to proceed on a purely speculative basis. Most financing requires some level of presales or preleasing before construction financing is triggered. Financing draws are usually tied to performance standards related to the sales/lease agreements secured as a percentage of the total to be developed.

Often real estate projects include a combination of speculative and nonspeculative development. For example, regional shopping center projects try to lock in "anchor" tenants on long-term leases. The remaining space devoted to small shops is rented as it becomes available. Securing major tenants is critical to success. Many national franchise operations seeking new retail outlets will automatically want to rent space in any center with a particular anchor or combination of anchor tenants. The development of a market capture strategy results in two different outcomes. The strategy must develop a pricing schema that facilitates sale or lease of the available space. Secondly, the strategy must consider the physical layout, the unit sizes, exterior and interior amenities, and other special features designed to assure strong demand for the units. Even in very active, growing markets the market capture strategy can spell the difference between success and failure.

Of course, a good marketing strategy must also recognize best-case and worst-case scenarios. These scenarios are translated into various absorption rates as project space comes onto the market. Typically, the developer knows how much revenue must be generated each month, at a minimum, to meet expenses and obligations and how to proceed if revenues fall below minimum levels.

In summary, the real estate market study considers regional, area-wide, industry-specific, indirect site-specific, and direct site-specific economic conditions and trends. It uses this information to project demand for space in one or more categories: retail, office, manufacturing, hotels, and so forth. By surveying existing facilities and planned projects, supply is forecast and comparable developments are identified. A careful relative assessment of supply and demand leads to determining whether the identified project can be accepted by the market and of whether particular segments of the market are underserved. The critical phase involves developing a market strategy that designs the real estate space to be supplied based on market capture, sets the prices, sets absorption rates for the space provided, and determines how the units will be promoted and sold or leased. The price information forms the basis of the financial feasibility analysis.[2]

EXAMPLES OF REAL ESTATE MARKET ANALYSIS

The examples describe a retail project, an office project, and an industrial project. The projects are hypothetical.

The LDO market study for downtown retail space began with a discussion of the appropriate trade area. The decision was made to define the trade area as the entire county.[3] The next task was to examine retailing trends. Over the past decade, the expenditures of county residents on shoppers goods (that is, apparel, furniture, appliances, and major purchases) grew from $650 million to $950 million. Expenditures on convenience goods (that is, food, drugs, eating, drinking, and other minor purchases) grew at a similar rate, from $1,800 million to $2,600 million. The retail sales of the county represented expenditures of both county residents and nonresidents. These sales figures amounted to 50 percent of expected resident expenditures for shoppers goods and 75 percent of expected resident expenditures for convenience goods. These percentages had grown modestly over the past decade. During this period, the downtown area captured 10 percent and 25 percent of the total county expenditures for shoppers goods and convenience goods, respectively.

LDO staff made projections of supply and demand. Although county population and income were expected to grow by over 30 percent in the next ten years, the market study concluded that no new retail space was needed in the downtown area. One major factor came from the industry-specific study. Off-price retail outlets were on the rise, and several were planned along major highways to the east and west of the county. These projects appeared capable of absorbing almost all of the growth in shoppers goods, and projections indicated the county's share of shoppers goods expenditures would drop sharply. Downtown merchants were going to lose sales and face difficult times in the future.

The picture for convenience goods was brighter. The county and downtown shares were expected to decline modestly, but because the level of expenditures was growing, total downtown sales were expected to grow slightly. A survey of sales projects of downtown merchants selling convenience goods led to the conclusion that their projections were too optimistic. Given planned expansions of existing businesses and several approved projects, new retail projects supplying additional space were clearly infeasible in the downtown area.

As a result, local officials commissioned a study of the retailing functions that could be offered downtown on a competitive basis in the rapidly changing environment. The study concluded that the downtown area could serve as an entertainment center. More restaurants, bars, and specialized food and gift shops could be better supported if more people lived and worked in or near the downtown area. Local officials incorporated this advice into the city's economic development strategy. Over the next three years, residential infill projects were encouraged, and retail projects were discouraged.

One area that looked very promising was additional office development. The then-existing share of total county office space located in the downtown area was only 10 percent, and several downtown sites were available.

The LDO staff began the market study with a survey of all major office buildings in the area. The results indicated very low vacancy rates (less than 2 percent), rental ranges and sales prices for this space, the unit size ranges, and the tenant profiles. Professionals—doctors, dentists, lawyers, accountants, management consultants, engineers, architects—occupied most of the rental units. Apparently, financial intermediaries, insurance companies, real estate firms, and government agencies were located in owner-occupied facilities. The LDO staff used industry projections for the county done by the Bureau of Economic Analysis and national occupational projections from the Bureau of Labor Statistics to arrive at estimates of growth in professional employment. Conservatively estimated, the space demand over the next ten years showed significant growth. The review of existing and proposed office projects from the survey indicated that the supply of office space would be considerably below anticipated demand. Over the next three years, excess demand was projected at 550,000 sq ft (2,500 new professionals requiring 220 sq ft on average).

A developer who owned a downtown office building and had control over an adjacent site was considering the development of a new office project. After carefully reviewing the market study, he estimated a capture rate, collected information on development and operating costs, and proposed a project of 120,000 sq ft. He began to formulate a marketing strategy at once. He planned to lease the space before and during the construction phase and to develop the project in three sequential phases, reflecting the absorption rates that were based on the increase in space demand over the next three years. The figures which follow pertain to the first phase of the project:

Lease Analysis

Revenues: Leasable office space of 40,000 sq ft @ $14.00 per sq ft	$560,000
less: vacancy/collection losses @ 10%	56,000
Gross operating income	504,000
less: operating expenses @ 35%	176,400
Net operating income	327,600

Development costs

Hard costs

Land and improvements	350,000
Office space: 45,000 sq ft (89% efficient to yield 40,000 sq ft leasable) @ $28 per sq ft	1,260,000
Contingency @ 10% of hard costs	161,000
Soft costs @ 24% of hard costs	390,000
Total development costs	2,161,000

Financing costs

Project value at 13% capitalization rate	2,520,000
Total development costs	2,161,000
Mortgage available @ 80% of development costs	1,728,800
Equity required	432,200
Debt service: principal amortized quarterly over 20 years @ 14% annual interest (10-year call provision)	258,524
Net cash flow: net operating income less debt service	69,076
Net cash flow as percent of equity	16.0%

The preliminary financial feasibility analysis looked very encouraging. Considering return on invested quity and project risks, the developer was very confident that the project could generate almost $70,000 in net cash flow annually. The more detailed financial feasibility analysis included other factors that increased equity return without increasing risk (as described in Chapter 7): gradual increase of net operating income over the next ten years as operating income rose faster than operating expenses; actual development costs of no more than $2.16 million and probably less; anticipation that the project would be sold within ten years, before the call provision was exercised; appreciation in the value of the property to generate capital gains of about $250,000; and tax benefits derived from deduction of mortgage interest and depreciation expensed on a straight-line basis.

In addition, the risks inherent in the project appeared quite manageable. The market for professional office space was strong. The real estate was expected to appreciate at about the inflation rate. The 14 percent mortgage interest rate, although high, was committed for ten years. The strong market allowed selling of the investment to local investors or conversion to office condominiums. The project did not appear to be overly exposed to legal, natural, or political risks.

The other project pursued in the downtown area was development of an industrial "incubator" facility. The inspiration for this project came from several sources. First, a researcher at the state university issued a report on "R & D incubator facilities" that were being developed around the country. The researcher indicated that the idea should be considered seriously for local application. Second, economic trends in the county and in the larger metropolitan area projected favorable changes in the area's industrial and occupation mixes. With new industries and households, changes in technology and tastes could make the area more fertile for new company formation. Finally, the local development organization had an option on an appropriate tract of partly vacant and underutilized land on the edge of the downtown area that was zoned for industry.

The first step of the market study involved identifying potential tenants for an incubator project. The essential idea was that entrepreneurs in the region were developing new products for the market. Some needed inexpensive space for periods of one to three years to develop prototypes and initiate production of limited quantities of product. If their businesses were successful, they would move to larger facilities, add employees, and produce at a larger scale. Other new entrepreneurs could establish themselves by selling R & D support services to growing companies located in the region.

To reach this potential market, LDO staff purchased subscription lists for the area, identified by ZIP codes, from several national magazines read by those contemplating new ventures. A questionnaire was designed and mailed to these individuals. The questionnaire stressed confidentiality and the benefits to them and to the community from a successful incubator project. The response was very disappointing. Besides a low response rate, only a few individuals indicated interest in renting space in an incubator facility.

The decision was made to redefine the project as a facility for local manufacturers and distributors who needed more space to carry out expansion plans. Since these companies were easy to locate, LDO staff conducted telephone interviews to get their reaction to the proposed project. Two sources of demand emerged. First, several companies expressed interest in moving into a new facility. Other firms were in desperate need of warehouse space.

A developer came forward with a project idea that provided space for two or three light manufacturers, space for the warehousing of inventories, offices for his clerical, secretarial, and bookkeeping staff, and office space to accommodate a few independent attorneys and accountants. The ideas were formalized in a preliminary site plan and project description. The local development organization reviewed the plan favorably.

The developer considered the project to be a risky one but believed that someone else would seize the opportunity if he failed to act expeditiously. Therefore, he formulated a worst-case scenario for the project and used the results to guide his marketing efforts to find tenants and to attract financing to the project. This analysis is summarized below.

Site acquisiion and improvements: approximately two acres	$150,000
Hard construction costs: 40,000 sq ft @ $15	600,000
Soft development costs	180,000
Total development costs	$930,000
Mortgage loan assuming loan-to-cost ratio of 0.80	744,000
Annual debt service assuming prevailing terms of financing	112,000
Equity required	186,000

Annual cash throw-off assuming before-tax return of 8%	15,000
Net operating income required to service debt and equity	127,000
Debt service coverage ratio acceptable to lenders	1.25
Minimum net operating income required by lenders	140,000
Expected operating expenses	55,000
Expected annual improvements	5,000
Required effective gross operating income	200,000
Expected vacancy or collection loss factor	0.05
Required gross revenues	210,500
Leasable space available (sq ft)	34,000
Average annual rent required per square foot	$6.19

The developer's decision focused on whether he could rent the space for an average price of $6.19/sq ft. At a cost below $6.00/sq ft, the project would be extremely attractive to light industry. However, that price was still too high for warehouse space. Thus, the demand for warehousing could not be met.

The developer began advertising for tenants seeking 10,000–15,000 sq ft of space for manufacturing. The asking rent was $6.00/sq ft. The space was to be available in 10–12 months. Based upon the ad, a pre-lease agreement was signed for 12,000 sq ft at $6.00 for a two-year lease term. With this agreement in hand, the developer was able to attract private and public funds to the project. The rest of the space was divided into smaller units and rented for $7.00/sq ft, on average.

BUSINESS DEVELOPMENT PROJECTS

Many business development projects present no difficulties in determining economic feasibility. For some businesses, the markets to be served are well known, and these businesses have active accounts that will generate the anticipated sales. In other instances, private participants are fully capable of determining economic feasibility. The public's role is limited to review of the business plan to judge whether to participate in the project.

However, market and feasibility analysis will be of central importance for other potential public–private ventures such as for business starts and for certain acquisitions and expansions that represent the development of new products and the pursuit of new markets. In these instances, the proposed project should be analyzed separately from existing profit centers of the going concern. For simplicity the following discussion is cast in terms of start-up projects.

Business starts involving joint participation can serve local or nonlocal markets. Most retailing, personal services, contract construction, and some business and professional services have local markets. For these sectors, the market study and financial feasibility analysis follow the methods and procedures used to analyze real estate projects quite closely. Logically, the decision to provide space for local businesses is predicated on the determination that these businesses will grow and prosper in the area and therefore will be seeking space. A market must support more shoppers-goods retailers, for example, to provide space that will be utilized profitably by these retailers. However, the real estate investment decision is more general in that *some* retailer must be able to exploit the market. The small business investment decision determines if one particular retailer can operate in the market successfully.

For locally oriented starts the step that is equivalent to defining the uses of space in real estate projects is defining the business—the goods or services to be provided. Site selection and market or trade area identification are the next and most critical steps. Within this trade area, the competition must be analyzed and a market capture strategy developed. As a result, market share and sales volume can be projected over time. Based on sales revenue estimates, pro forma financials are prepared to determine feasibility.

For businesses oriented to nonlocal markets, the approach is somewhat different. The exporting business must define the nonlocal market for its products more precisely in terms of a listing of the potential customers of the new business.[4] The most useful way to start this process is to identify the competition and move from there to an analysis of the market and of financial feasibility.

The tasks involved in the market study for the company serving nonlocal markets may be summarized as follows:

- Definition of the business—the goods or services to be produced
- Analysis of competing businesses
- Identification of clients/customers
- Projection of sales volume generated by existing and potential customer base
- Estimation of competitors' sales volumes and a feasible share of the market

● Development of a market capture strategy

● Projection of sales volumes over time at expected levels and at conservative levels

With these results, drawing up the financials is relatively straight-forward. While nonlocal conditions drive the market study, local economic and political conditions are the ones that determine the start-up costs and the costs of normal operations. Usually, income statements and balance sheets for three years are developed, as are an initial sources and uses of funds statement and a cash-flow statement for at least the first 12 months of operations.

The LDO director should encourage the entrepreneur to analyze economic feasibility as part of the business planning process. The difference between success and failure usually depends on the entrepreneur's ability to develop a sound market capture strategy and to secure the necessary accounts. New ventures fail most often because of inadequate marketing and sales effort and less frequently due to production and operational problems. Successful marketing reflects both the soundness of the business proposal and the capability of the person(s) running the business.

Market studies for new business development should be made as accurate and objective as possible. The points presented below are helpful suggestions gleaned from the literature on economic feasibility analysis. (See the citations listed under Business Development in the Bibliography.)

The analysis of the competition should be thorough. Not only is the market identified from this analysis but so are the main strengths and weaknesses of competitors. The unique capabilities of the business relative to the competition informs a thoughtful market capture strategy. (What will be done differently compared to competitors, to win over new accounts? Which market segments appear most attractive?)

The market analyst should avoid using what might be called supply-side approaches to projecting sales. For example, one approach used to estimate sales is to multiply the value of assets by the turnover ratio (sales per dollar of assets). Another approach multiplies square footage to be developed by an average sales figure to get estimated sales. The assumption behind these approaches is that sales can be generated by simply supplying assets or space. This microlevel version of Say's Law appears as questionable as its macrolevel counterpart. Sales estimates should be based on the joint consideration of demand and supply and on potential market share, given competitors' strategies.

Sales forecasts should not necessarily be based on the assumption of stable prices. In constant dollar terms, prices can fall or rise. An analysis of the historical experience for the class of commodity under study can be very helpful. Also, an application of the learning curve concept posits a negative relationship between prices and volume (see Lee 1978, Ch. 7). While more appropriate to a single business entity, average prices in the industry may drop as the cumulative number of units sold increases over time.

Although financials should be drafted using cost estimates that reflect local market conditions, sources of financial characteristics of specific businesses do exist and can be used to make comparisons to budgets developed for the new venture (for example, Robert Morris & Associates income statements, the Almanac of Business and Industrial Financial Ratios).[5] A somewhat different approach is "the financial reality test." This approach is used to estimate the level of sales required to meet the entrepreneur's earnings expectations. The approach considers salary requirements, return-on-investment objectives, and reinvestment needs to generate a projection of required sales (see Schweser 1982, p. 80). Finally, break-even analysis is often utilized to examine sales required to justify an investment. One form of the relationship is as follows: $BE = FC + P/(1 - VC/S)$, where BE is the break-even sales level; FC is the total fixed costs; P is the profit level set equal to zero; VC is the total variable costs; and S is the sales volume corresponding to the level of VC. Various applications of this formula are concisely explained in the *Business Owner*, 1983.

EXAMPLES OF BUSINESS DEVELOPMENT MARKET ANALYSIS

The examples present the marketing questions addressed in three new ventures—a retail business, a processing/wholesaling business, and a small manufacturing business.

An independent grocer contacted the cooperative from which she purchased standard brands to develop a market study for a new store to replace her existing operation. The coop's store location analyst contacted a West Coast firm specializing in the compilation of spatial information. The firm had 1980 census information on file for all block groups and enumeration districts in the country. For each spatial unit, the spatial distribution of resident population was used to calculate a center point which represented the mean or weighted average location of population. The mean center point is called the centroid. The firm defined trade areas from any point by drawing concentric circles at increasing distances from that point. All spatial units with centroids on or within the circumference were included in that trade area. The firm provided a detailed printout of demographic characteristics for the primary, secondary, and tertiary trade areas at four, eight, and twelve miles. The information included population count, households by size distribution, household income, race, age, occupation, education, vehicles by household, labor force participation, and housing characteristics.

The store location analyst determined that the eight-mile perimeter included most of the market area, given the area's population and employment patterns and the general nature of the proposed business. The next step involved using detailed expenditure figures to arrive at total expenditures for all merchandise. The per capita expenditure figures included food items, such as cereal products, poultry, fresh fruits, fats and oils, beverages, and other merchandise including drugs, housekeeping supplies, and tobacco products. The total weekly sales potential came to $15.70 per capita. The 21,500 people within eight miles of the proposed site were spending about $337,500 per week on grocery store merchandise.

The next step involved modifying these estimates to account for future trends. The utility company serving the area was contacted and agreed to provide information on the 1980 level of accounts and changes since that time. Based on these figures and population projections made by the state budget office, the population within the market area was expected to grow modestly over time. A national trade organization for food stores was asked to provide projections of household expenditures for food and other merchandise. Although the distribution of expenditures was changing, the overall level was predicted to remain stable in constant dollar terms for the next several years. The changing expenditure patterns provided useful information subsequently in developing the market capture plan for the business.

Not content with these secondary sources of information, the grocer conducted a household survey with help from a class at the nearby community college. The one-in-twenty survey of 1,400 households living in the area immediately adjacent to the site included information on household size and total weekly expenditures on food to be prepared at home and on related merchandise. Based on the results of this random sample, the grocer decided to lower the total weekly sales potential to $14.50. The estimated market potential for the next five years was calculated as follows:

Year	Population	Potential Sales ($)
1	21,500	311,750
2	21,715	314,868
3	21,932	318,016
4	22,151	321,190
5	22,373	324,409

The most difficult task was determining a reasonable market share for the new facility. First, the competition in or near the market area was identified, including the grocer's existing operation. Stores 1 and 2 were branches of large chains. Store 3 was a small independent. Store 4 was the grocer's existing facility. Based on conversations with the store managers, local bankers, regional equipment suppliers, and grocers in other nearby market areas, the following figures were compiled:

Store	Location	Size (sq ft)	Estimated weekly sales volume ($)
1	shopping center	15,000	75,000
2	shopping center	10,000	40,000
3	downtown	4,000	10,000
4	downtown	10,000	25,000

The two chain stores were realizing $5.00 and $4.00 of weekly sales per square foot, but the independents were averaging $2.50. The total sales volume of these food stores was $150,000 weekly, about 48% of the existing market.

Based on a review of all projects under consideration by the planning board and discussions with local realtors handling commercial properties, no additional grocers were expected to come into the market area. However, store 2 could expand at its current location.

The grocer believed that the two chain stores would be able to capture 46 percent of the market in five years by adding 5,000 sq ft of capacity and averaging sales of $5.00/sq ft on the total of 30,000 sq ft. The other independent grocer was expected to retire in a few years, and the facility would probably be put to another use. Given this situation, how much of the market could be captured by the new facility?

If all stores serving the households in the market area captured 50 percent of their total expenditures, then on average over the next five years about $159,000 of weekly sales would be realized. Even with Store 3 out of business, the chains were expected to capture $150,000, leaving only $9,000 per week for another store. This analysis clearly indicated that a feasible project would depend on a site development plan, store layout, and marketing strategy that would increase the percentage of total market area expenditures captured by local facilities.

Based on an analysis of the competition in and near the market area, the grocer decided to propose a 15,000-sq ft facility that had many innovative features—specialty foods, fresh foods, a bakery—to attract new customers to the facility. By subdividing the square footage into several profit centers, the grocer was able to estimate an average sales per square foot and average weekly sales volume. The figures were $4.00 and $60,000. This sales volume required a substantial 19 percent of the total market or a 66 percent share of the $318,000 market for the three facilities.

The analysis indicated that the proposed new facility was too ambitious. Moreover, although the start-up costs for fixed assets and inventories were manageable, the amount of working capital required for advertising, debt service, and other fixed expenses far exceeded the grocer's cash reserves. As a result, she and her banker agreed that the project was too risky. Instead, she decided to modify her existing operation to introduce a bakery and a specialty foods center. If she were able to increase sales per square foot to $3.50 over the next year, she would again consider developing a new food center.

The coffee-roasting business described in Chapter 7 developed a marketing plan by completing the analysis summarized below. With a small-scale processing and wholesaling operation, variable expenses were reasonably expected to be about 70 percent of sales. Fixed costs at the proposed site were estimated at $27,000 annually. Break-even sales were calculated as follows:

$$BE = FC + P/(1 - VC/S)$$
$$= \$27,000 + 0/(1 - 0.70)$$
$$= \$27,000/0.30 = \$90,000$$

Mr. Dane began the market study by defining 250 miles as the maximum reasonable trip to maintain timely deliveries and a fresh product. This market area included over 200 good restaurants and about 30 quality hotels. He began attending meetings where restaurant managers came together to examine new equipment and discuss other shared concerns. Through these contacts he developed a mailing list of over 100 restaurants.

Next, he sent a letter to each describing the product. He offered to develop a unique blend of coffee for that restaurant, supply the coffee in bean form or in predosed packages, and deliver the product several times weekly. Follow-up conversations with respondents indicated that he could sell about 600 pounds annually to the average customer at a price of $5.00–$5.60/lb. About 20 restaurants appeared to be interested in the product at this price, but the venture could not break even with these 20 prospects as the only customers:

Sales from 20 restaurants × 600 lbs @ $5.30/lb	$63,600
less: variable expenses	44,520
	19,080
less: fixed costs	27,000
Profit	-7,920

Break-even volume was about 17,000 pounds of coffee annually, or about 28 customers. Mr. Dane decided to seek advance orders from at least 30 customers and to test the response to lower price levels before going ahead with the new venture.

Compared to the grocer serving a local market and the coffee wholesaler selling to a regional market, a would-be manufacturer of hydraulic cylinders sought to sell his product throughout North America. As a production manager for a farm equipment manufacturer, he learned that quality hydraulic cylinders were often hard to find. Preliminary research indicated that a relatively small number of large companies purchased the product from a large number of small producers.

He believed demand would grow over the next decade for large cylinders (over ten feet long) for use in mining, construction, and specialized transportation equipment. Although prospects in his own industry did not seem bright, growth was expected in major national firms concentrated in other sectors.

He decided to leave his position, live on his savings, and devote a year to finding accounts for large hydraulic cylinders. After three months of extensive travel, he had identified ten firms that were interested in purchasing large cylinders over the next several years. The annual sales volume generated by these accounts was expected to be just over $1.0 million.

At the same time, an associate was developing pro forma financials on the new business. The analysis indicated that an efficient facility with about 25 employees would have a break-even sales volume of about $700,000.

Encouraged by these results, the entrepreneur approached a national business development company with his preliminary business plan. The key element was the prospective account list that identified each firm, gave the estimated annual sales potential, and listed the name and telephone number of the company's contact person. The loan officer was able to corroborate the sales estimates. A more detailed business plan was developed subsequently. The business development company accepted the plan and began the initial financing of the new venture.

The bibliography on market and feasibility analysis includes general references, as well as references on real estate feasibility studies and small business feasibility studies. These readings provide additional operational details for designing and evaluating market and feasibility studies. Also, Appendix E gives an overview of two market studies, one completed for a real estate development project and the other for a business development project.

What should be emphasized, in conclusion, is the uncertainty and complexity that surrounds the appraisal of local real estate and business development projects. Having developers/entrepreneurs, investors, and lenders in honest disagreement over the economic feasibility of identified projects is not uncommon. Particularly in these instances, the local development organization should be prepared to sponsor its own market study and feasibility analysis. These studies can help the public sector make a sound decision about whether to participate in a local development project.

NOTES

1. Many industries such as communications and financial services are undergoing fundamental changes which are driven by changes in government regulatory and tax policy, corporate investment planning, and the introduction of new technologies. Generally these changes have enlarged market areas and heightened the competition for local markets.

2. Before moving to examples of market and feasibility analysis for real estate projects, the boundary that separates real estate projects from business development projects can be described. The key parameters are the number of space users, the specificity of space use, and the importance of space use. The typical real estate project creates general-purpose space that can be occupied by many different businesses and used for several different functions. The typical business development project seeks to implement a particular business plan that incidentally includes space requirements. Two strategies for supporting local manufacturing growth are presented below as examples of each type of project.

The industrial recruitment and promotion strategy described in Chapter 3 is frequently tied to the development of an industrial park which offers sites for new manufacturing facilities. By providing roads, infrastructure, and related amenities that meet the expectations of the national clients, the sites can be made attractive to companies engaged in a wide range of industrial activities. Industrial park sites are marketed through the industrial location specialists and property management officers of major companies.

On the other hand, the strategy that supports the expansion of existing industries focuses attention on a few local companies with specific business plans and particular space needs. Often expansion can be accomplished by adding equipment and personnel without increasing space consumption. In other situations, more space is required and a dedicated facility is usually built.

Small manufacturers usually seek to exercise site control. They often find it convenient to lease their facility from the company owner(s). In this way, the company has an adequate, reliable facility, and the owner is able to apply the real estate tax benefits against personal income.

3. Primary, secondary, and tertiary trade areas can be defined around any site at increasing distances from the site. Most market studies focus on primary trade areas using county, township, or, in larger cities, census tract boundaries.

4. New businesses selling to nonlocal markets serve other businesses or government agencies. Besides small mail-order houses, most businesses selling to households nationally are very large companies. Small local businesses that achieve great success selling to households usually grow by opening new units near the original location. Sometimes the new entities are organized as subsidiary operations. More frequently, franchising is used to propagate the successful business concept.

5. One of the main differences between real estate and business feasibility pertains to the accounting basis and financial accounts used. Real estate projects are reckoned on a cash-flow basis; business financials are reckoned on an accrual basis, as noted in Chapter 5.

9

THE NATIONAL PERSPECTIVE ON LOCAL DEVELOPMENT

The last four chapters have provided a detailed introductory treatment of project planning and management required to effectively design, evaluate, finance, and carry out local public–private ventures and co-development projects. To be deemed politically and economically feasible and to attract adequate financing, these projects must meet both public economic development objectives and market tests. The strategic and theoretical perspectives developed in the first four chapters offer the broader understanding of economic development that is needed to articulate and pursue a balanced public–private approach to local development. These strategic-level and project-level concepts should encourage more meaningful local economic development efforts. However, we must take a final look at local economic development from a broader perspective to assess properly local economic development strategies and public economic development objectives.

Local economies collectively form the system of cities and regions that constitute the international economy. The spatial and temporal relationships between places are manifestations of the form and pace of economic development.[1] National policy makers should recognize the importance and integrity of local economies which collectively form the national economy as part of the global economic system. Spatial differentiation in economic functions and institutions deserves consideration that goes well beyond the debates about moving jobs to people or people to jobs. Local economic development is integral, not incidental, to national economic growth and development.

Local policy makers should pursue opportunities to contribute to national and international development. They should resist mercantile positions and zero-sum strategies even if they are politically popular. Local development professionals should support local policy makers and stress the need to pursue positive-sum efforts. In an economic system that is highly interdependent, parochial public aims and strategies will retard local economic development over the long term more often than not.

From a broader perspective, the first requirement of local economic development efforts is that they contribute to national economic well-being. Many conventional approaches to economic development do not meet this criterion. Some local efforts, such as industrial recruitment and promotion, serve mainly to redistribute investment from one locality to another without creating new jobs or wealth for the system as a whole. Although recruitment efforts can provide better information to corporate planners and facilitate the investment process, many states and localities go far beyond modest forms of assistance. Inter-area competition for corporate investment has become very intense, and the public costs are very high for the nation as a whole (see Goodman 1979, Miller 1983).

The federal government should encourage and reward cooperation among state and local jurisdictions in locating corporate facilities. It could restrict or eliminate some of the tools that are used to bid for corporate investments. Although based on federal tax loss grounds, moves to limit the amount of revenue bonds issued by states is one example of such action. Other potential targets include restrictions on land and facility grants, tax incentives, and regulatory relief offered locally. In turn the federal government could reduce federal tax expenditures designed to encourage corporate investment but which also increase its spatial mobility. The investment tax credit is a leading candidate in this area.[2]

From a national perspective, other local economic development strategies, while appearing to be productive, may yield a constant-sum effect on the national economy. Many localities articulate strategies that result in either export promotion or import substitution. Local export promotion and import substitution activities can contribute to national economic growth when factor inputs are used more productively or new products and processes are developed. However, when substitution and replacement occur, these activities result in gains and losses that are compensating among areas. Such constant-sum activities are irrational from the national perspective because all areas cannot simultaneously increase exports and reduce imports. In this regard, mercantile and protectionist policies advocated at the national level set an unfortunate example for states and localities.

Export diversification is open to the same criticism as export promotion and import substitution when it fails to introduce innovations. One area may be able to improve its balance of trade in the short term by producing a broader mix of products for export. Yet if all areas pursue this strategy, export diversification will result in lower export prices and less favorable terms of trade for all exporting areas in the long term.

Thus, local professionals and policy makers should look closely at local economic development strategies to define alternatives that can improve the local economy and enhance national economic well-being. The pursuit of a positive-sum portfolio of local strategies is no more difficult than the pursuit of beggar-thy-neighbors strategies. Yet it should be far more sustaining and rewarding over the long term.

Usually local economic development activities are justified for the purposes of job creation and tax revenue enhancement. While these objectives are reasonable, there is a potential conflict between the objectives of more jobs and larger tax base. Local actors concerned about property values and other stocks of local wealth (for example, local bankers, insurance and utility company executives, real estate brokers and developers, and large landowners) support the tax revenue objective and co-development efforts because they promise to increase asset values. On the other hand, local actors representing industrial, labor, and neighborhood groups favor job creation. As noted in Chapter 3, business starts, expansions, and acquisitions have the greatest impact on job creation and retention.

Given limited public resources, conflicts may occur when choosing between co-development projects and public–private business development projects. Will the locality emphasize employment or tax base? To some extent this conflict is mitigated by the fact that the objectives are not mutually exclusive. Many business development projects include real estate development. A decision to finance one type of project first does not preclude the option of financing the other type of project later. Proceeds from loans to businesses, for example, can be used to finance public improvements or tax-base enhancing projects.

More importantly, conflicts between these objectives can be mitigated by appealing to other objectives that support national economic growth and development to which the objectives of job creation and tax base enhancement can be subordinated. Economic development objectives derived from the perspective of entrepreneurship theories discussed in Chapter 3 provide the best case in point. Innovation, product development, and productivity improvements are the central concerns from this perspective.

Similarly, business development strategies are more or less consistent with the goal of improving national economic well-being. Alternatives that support innovation, product development, and productivity improvements are the best. At the local level, encouraging entrepreneurship, new business formation, and the expansion of existing industries are superior strategies. Retooling facilities and retraining workers to stabilize existing industries and the acquisition of viable economic entities abandoned by conglomerates or retiring founders are also strategically sound. From the national perspective, local strategies designed primarily to avoid business contractions or plant closures, or to interfere with the diffusion of corporate facilities are inferior alternatives.

With policies, strategies, and projects formulated in the national interest, local economic development practice will move in several possible directions. One possibility is that public economic development objectives and private wealth-creating objectives will coincide sufficiently to sustain the growth of public–private ventures and co-development projects. In this instance, the trend that has emerged recently will continue and possibly accelerate over the next decade. A second possibility is that public and private objectives will diverge, requiring a distinct and separate role for local government. At one extreme, local governments may choose to finance government enterprises to compete in product markets and encourage public ownership to alter control of factor markets. At the other extreme, local governments may return to financing traditional public investments, vesting private enterprise with the task of planning and directing the economic development process.

NOTES

1. Jane Jacobs presents a global perspective on local economic development in refreshing and challenging terms (see Jacobs 1984).

2. Of course, this position begs the larger question concerning the extent to which corporate activities should be taxed relative to non-corporate sources of tax revenues.

EXERCISES

Exercise 1: Think about the local economy with which you are concerned. Who is planning work for this area? What planners are most important in terms of their local economic impacts? Who is local/nonlocal? Is anyone creating new local companies or new opportunities for doing work?

Draw a chart of the interorganization that influences local economic development in your area. Who are the key actors (the planners)? Locate key actors in the interorganization. Where does your organization fit into this picture? How do you relate to these key actors? How could you better relate to them in order to influence their plans?

Exercise 2: Either alone or with a small group of staff members, devote about one hour to brainstorming, following the rules given in the text. Identify environmental/contingent events. Choose one event. Continue brainstorming to generate lists of impacts, responses, and results.

In the next hour develop a first-cut plan in the form of two short essays (scenarios) about this event, its impacts, your responses to the event, and the different results. In the first half hour, develop a *success* story with respect to results. Does the first scenario help to better understand your aims and purposes? In the last half hour, develop a *failure* story with respect to results. Does the second scenario help to realize what could go wrong and improve your responses (that is, improve your strategy or contingency plan)?

Exercise 3: Review economic base theory as summarized in the text and as discussed in Appendix A. From this theoretical perspective, write a definition of local economic development, the strategy that you prefer for promoting local economic development in your locality according to this definition, and the most effective role that you can play to carry out this strategy. List the local groups likely to benefit from this strategy and those likely to be hurt by it.

Exercise 4: Review the materials in Appendix B. Write down a definition of economic development compatible with this material. Write a concise strategy to promote local economic development as you have defined it and the role that you would like to play to carry out this strategy.

Exercise 5: From the perspective of the organization with which you are affiliated and in the context of the community with which you are concerned, what is the best definition of local economic development that you can suggest? What is the second-best definition?

Exercise 6: Review the business development strategies in Chapter 3. Considering your organization's strengths and weaknesses, describe an optimal portfolio of strategies. Be sure that the strategies are desirable from your organization's standpoint and that the approach is feasible given your understanding of the local economy. List the tools needed to achieve each strategy. How will you modify the strategies and tools that you want to employ if the resources at your disposal for economic development activities are cut by 50 percent? Increased by 50 percent?

Exercise 7: Draw a table with key local actors identified forming the rows and economic development tools forming the columns. Which tools are being used by each actor? Describe briefly the role each could play to pursue a desirable economic or business development strategy. Focus on your role. What is the most appropriate role for you to play in promoting local economic/business development?

Exercise 8: Refer to Exercises 4 through 7. Do you have to specify further the definition of business development to successfully administer a local business development fund? If not, why not? If so, can you use the definition developed in Exercise 5 to come up with specific objectives for the uses of funds? Can you add any rules to help achieve your objectives and better define the uses of funds? Can you identify eligibility requirements or criteria? If so, list them. If not, explain your reasons for not having them.

Exercise 9: Assume that the business development fund had $1.0 million in capitalization, $400,000 in deposits and $600,000 in contributions. You have identified enough worthwhile local projects to absorb 80 percent of the fund's resources. The rest of the capitalization is to remain in low-risk securities. Annual costs include $50,000 for fund administration and an 8 percent simple interest rate paid on deposits. Security investments are expected to generate an effective annual yield of 11 percent. What average effective interest rate will have to be charged on loans to local projects to have the fund break even for the year? If 5 percent of the loans are nonperforming, what average interest rate will have to be charged to break even? If the amounts of deposits and contributions were reversed, what average interest rate will have to be charged to break even with no nonperforming loans? With 5 percent nonperforming loans?

Exercise 10: Take a local economic development project with which you are familiar and for which documentation is available. After reviewing Exercise 5, adapt the Economic Development Checklist to suit your purposes. Score the project using the adapted checklist.

If time permits, repeat the exercise to evaluate another project.

Exercise 11: Using the information given below for a hypothetical company, compute the applicable financial ratios listed in Appendix D.

Balance Sheets (in $1,000)

	December 31, 1980	December 31, 1981
Cash	100	50
Accounts receivable	500	550
Inventories	1,800	1,600
Current assets	2,400	2,200
Fixed assets	1,400	1,300
Other assets (marketable securities)	200	200
Total assets	4,000	3,700
Current liabilities	1,300	1,000
Long-term liabilities	1,100	1,000
Stock and paid-in capital	1,000	1,000
Retained earnings	600	700
Total liabilities	4,000	3,700

Income Statement for the Year 1981 (in $1,000)

Sales	7,500
less: cost of goods sold	5,200
Gross margin	2,300
less: operating expenses	1,200
Earnings before interest and taxes	1,100
less: interest	200
taxes	400
Net profit	500

Statement of Retained Earnings (in $1,000)

Retained earnings 12/31/80	600
add: net profit, 1981	500
	1,100
less: dividends paid	400
Retained earnings 12/31/81	700

Write a description of the ABC company's financial structure using the computed ratios assuming that the norms listed in the appendix apply.

Exercise 12: XYZ Development Company has $2.0 million to invest in your community. They must earn 15 percent cash-on-cash rate of return to be interested in any local real estate project. Determine whether the company would want to invest in the real estate project described below.

Annual Income (in $1,000)

Gross leases	1,250
less: vacancy contingency	70
Effective gross rent	1,180
less: operating expenses	250
maintenance and repairs	50
insurance	25
property taxes	75
Net operating income	780
less: debt service	440
Net cash flow	340

Upon completion, the property will be appraised at $6.0 million. It can be developed at a cost of $5.0 million. Could the developer raise the necessary capital from local lenders to purchase the property if they required a loan coverage ratio of 0.6 and a debt coverage ratio of 1.5:1? Assume that these annual flows were expected to remain constant over time. Compute the annual capitalization rate for the project.

Exercise 13: Estimate balance sheets for 1986 and 1987 using the figures given in the Proposed Financing statement assuming: straight-line depreciation of all fixed assets; machinery and equipment valued at $24,000; real estate valued at $10,000 for land and $28,000 for buildings; machinery and equipment with five year economic life; and buildings with 15-year economic life.

Calculate the ten ratios discussed in the text using your estimates for 1986 and 1987.

Exercise 14: What rate of interest did the LDO charge to result in the 10 percent average cost of capital sought? Design the term and amortization of the LDO loan compatible with the uses of funds and business circumstances described.

Exercise 15: Using the growth-rate formula that includes the leverage ratio, change each of the following parameters individually and separately to generate a zero growth rate: *e*, *i*, *t*, and *d*. What is the growth rate with *L* equal to zero? Show how increasing leverage increases return on equity.

Taking 1984 as Year 1, calculate S & C's debt service for the first five years after the expansion. Assume a 12 percent prime rate throughout the period and 12 percent fixed interest being charged on $270,000 of existing debt. Total debt service will equal debt service on existing loans, on the new bank loan, and on the LDO loan. What would happen to net profit if S & C Corp.'s before-tax earnings dropped to $50,000 in Year 5? What minimum amount must the company earn each year during the five-year period in order to remain solvent?

Exercise 16: Fill in the amount of financing from each source of funds by reviewing the discussion in the text.

Exercise 17: Do you think that a reasonable price was paid for the acquisition? Show the amounts that you would have bid for each category of assets. Construct an opening balance sheet for the project to summarize these asset values and the sources of funds secured to finance them. Do a sensitivity analysis computing return on investment for different levels of total investment. How do these returns compare to expected return in the case study?

Exercise 18: Calculate the amount of LDO financing required. Prove that no positive rate of interest could be charged on a 30-year LDO loan of this principal amount.

Exercise 19: Assume that the development company has the capacity to do architectural and engineering studies, to market and sell leases, and to play the role of general contractor. What percentage of the estimated development costs would go to the development company?

With net operating income of $210,000 and desired return on total investment of 13.5 percent, compute the project's economic value. Given this estimate of value and a loan of $1,100,000, calculate the lender's exposure. At this principal amount and with the terms that are shown in the mortgage analysis, compute the debt service ratio for the first mortgage only.

Exercise 20: Assume that the property is sold after ten years at a price that reflects appreciation at a rate of 2 percent per annum from an initial replacement cost of $1,908,000. Further assume that selling expenses (brokerage commissions, closing costs, and so forth) are 6 percent of the sales price. Compute the outstanding balances on the two loans. Find the before-tax net proceeds of the sale.

Assuming that no improvements are made, the initial replacement cost is the basis of the property. From the cost basis, deduct accumulated depreciation expenses claimed for the first ten years in order to find the adjusted book value of the property. Compute the taxable gain which is the difference between net proceeds from the sale and the property's adjusted book value. Of this amount 40 percent is subject to income tax at 45 percent as long-term capital gains income. What amount of after-tax income is realized from the sale?

Note: Examples of correctly prepared responses to the exercises are available from the author.

APPENDIXES

A

DECISION THEORY AND
REGIONAL ECONOMIC GROWTH
P. Uathavikul

There is no theory or set of theories that adequately explains the complex process of regional growth and development. Several regional "theories" have been advanced in recent years for the study of regional problems, such as the stage theory, the sector theory, and the economic base (or export base) theory.

These theories have limitations of varying degree of severity, but they are all useful for descriptive or analytical purposes. From the point of view of the regional planner, however, their chief and common drawback is that they are not easily or readily translatable into normative models; and since the basic function of a planner is to draw up programs and recommend appropriate courses of action, this limitation is a serious one indeed.

Of the three approaches to the investigation of regional growth and development, the stage theory is the oldest. According to this approach, the course of growth and development in different regions may differ owing to peculiar local conditions, but there is a high degree of regularity and uniformity in the process itself. Furthermore, this process can be divided into fairly distinct stages of increasing complexity of organization in a "natural" or "normal" sequence. ... The explanatory variables are such growth factors as population increase and improvement in transportation and increasing specialization. The value of this approach is that it provides a unified framework for viewing the growth process through time, and can still give useful insights if applied with caution. Its major weaknesses are its over-simplification of the complex development process, the fundamental assumption of a unique growth path, and the difficulty of delineating the boundaries between the various stages.

Closely related to the stage theory is the sector theory, which holds that as growth and development take place, there tends to be an accompanying shift from the "lower" to the "higher" types of economic activity, specifically, from the primary through the secondary and on to the tertiary sectors. This shift is caused mainly by the different income elasticities of demand for the products of the sectors and changes in labor productivity. As income rises, the increase in demand for agricultural products will be less than that for industrial goods, and in the later stages of development, demand for industrial goods will be outstripped by demand for services. At the same time, because of technological improvement and increased capital investment, the same volume of primary and secondary products can be produced with less labor, while the possibility for factor substitution in the tertiary sector tends to be less significant. The main emphasis of this line of approach is, therefore, on internal changes and increasing specialization rather than external relationships. It focuses attention on internal structural relationships which are basic to the process of growth and development, such as those between income and consumption, technological change and factor productivity, and changes in factor availability and production. The major weaknesses of this theory are its neglect of interregional relationships and the very high degree of aggregation which it employs as a framework for analysis.

At the other extreme of emphasis is the export base model. The basic framework of this approach can be summarized as follows: the economic activities of a region can be divided into those which produce for the export market (basic industries) and those which produce for local regional market (nonbasic, service, or residentiary). The basic industries are assumed to be independent of the total structure of production of the region and are held to be the active "determinant" of regional growth, while residentiary industries are passive and are dependent on the "export base." If these assumptions are accepted, it would then be possible to use the basic-nonbasic ratio (employment, payrolls, etc.) to calculate a multiplier for estimating the changes in the regional economy due to changes in the export industries. Further, if this ratio is assumed to be constant through time, it can also be used to project future employment, or other appropriate economic magnitudes, from estimated changes in the export sector alone.

This theory points out the importance of external demand for the growth of a regional economy, but its limitations are obvious. Apart from the statistical difficulties in classifying the entire regional economy into basic and nonbasic sectors (owing to the shortcomings of statistical measures and the problem of intermediate products), the more serious weaknesses are: (a) the assumption that residentiary industries are passive or dependent upon the export base, when it is clear that internal changes constitute an important dynamic force in the process of growth, and that the nonbasic sector may play a decisive role in determining the extent of external trade through its influences on factor prices. Furthermore, the relative importance of external trade tends to vary with the size of the region and the stage of development of the economy; (b) the grossness of aggregation of the regional economy into only two sectors results in the suppression of inter-industry relations. The multiplier effects of export industries can vary widely, and the use of one multiplier can hardly be justified; (c) the analysis suppresses the importance of interregional relationships by treating all areas outside the region as one undifferentiated "rest of the world" sector; and, (d) there is no reason that the basic-nonbasic ratio will remain stable enough to serve as the fundamental relationship for prediction.

It was mentioned earlier that, from the point of view of the regional planner, the chief limitation of the approaches examined above is that they are not readily translatable into normative models for planning purposes. This fact can be illustrated by a brief discussion of what can easily happen to these theories when they are extended to cover some normative aspects of growth and development. Starting with stage theory, it has already been pointed out that this approach is now offered as a convenient framework for historical generalization, and it is useful for certain kinds of analysis as a system for organizing data. But, considering the present-day awareness of the large number of variables which enter into the growth and development process, there can be little doubt that no serious student of development would consider it as a workable guideline for action. A logical extension of the sector theory is the preoccupation, among local development groups, with the so-called "growth industries," i.e., those industries which have shown a greater rate of growth in employment or value added than the average rate will tend, *ceteris paribus*, to give the region a greater rate of growth than otherwise. But the crucial question is whether, given the input-output access of the region, it is the best possible alternative or even possible to attempt expanding or attracting these industries. The same difficulty arises in the extension of the export base theory. Even if it is accepted that the export sector is the "leading" sector of the regional economy, it does not necessarily follow that the most rapid rate of growth will be achieved by concentrating development efforts primarily on the export sector. Some indirect effects of external trade may, in fact, be harmful to the overall growth and development of the region, and in this respect, the controversy about the effects of trade on growth in the field of national economic development can be instructive. A satisfactory development program should be based on a careful study and evaluation of the export sector and its relation to the rest of the regional economy, as well as the benefits and possible disadvantages of trade. There are many and varied paths to growth, and a reasonable policy would appear to be one which pursued any combination of these paths which would yield the highest rate of growth consistent with the social and political objectives of society. An extension of the export base theory is too narrow in its exclusive emphasis on external relations, and is no help to the programmer in his attempt to identify the "right" combination of strategies and to solve the problem of resource allocation.

B

ENTREPRENEURSHIP: KEY TO SELF-RENEWING ECONOMIES

A. Shapero

The United States is rediscovering the critical importance of new firm formations to a self-renewing economy. Corporate failures during the last several years have raised questions about the efficacy of large organizations. And a series of recent studies have stressed the vital contribution of new, young firms to innovation and job growth in the nation.

A survey by the American Electronics Association, for example, revealed that firms from ten to 20 years old had 20 to 40 times the job growth rate of older firms; firms between five and ten years old— 55 times the job growth rate; and firms less than five years old— 115 times.

A National Science Foundation study concluded that small firms produced 24 times as many major innovations as large firms did and four times as many as medium-sized firms did. Small companies were also found to be more efficient producers of innovations, with a ratio of innovations to R&D employment four times that of large firms.

Large firms tend to be capital intensive and are engaged wherever possible in getting more done with fewer people, in substituting capital for labor, thus reducing the number of jobs. A good example is the current effort in the U.S. automobile industry to become more competitive through robots. Even when large firms are involved in mergers and acquisitions, they strive to reduce the number of employees required, including managers.

Furthermore, the bureaucratic behavior of large companies is typified by risk avoidance. There is a notable trend away from long-term research and development investments in large corporations, and increasing interest in acquiring smaller firms that have already taken the risk and developed both product and market. Yet what appears as a big risk for a very large firm, such as an apparent market

---

Reprinted from *Commentary* 5 (April 1981):19-23. Published by the National Council for Urban Economic Development.

Albert Shapero is William H. Davis Professor of The American Free Enterprise System at Ohio State University.

for only 100,000 units, is perceived by the small firm as an immense and golden opportunity.

COMMUNITY DYNAMISM

As we reassess our economic development policies, it is important to consider the special vulnerability of highly specialized industrial cities and regions versus the greater resilience of local and regional economies that contain large numbers of small firms.

Contrasting Manchester and Birmingham, England in the mid-nineteenth century, architectural writer and critic Jane Jacobs sought clues to long-term community dynamism. She pointed out that knowledgeable writers of the period extolled Manchester as a paragon of efficiency and model of the future. At that time, Britain dominated the world in textiles, and Manchester, located near the great port of Liverpool, was the heart of Britain's textile industry. The coal, necessary pure water and humid climate all made Manchester a natural hub of textile manufacturing. Supplementary and supporting industries, such as cotton-textile machinery and dye manufacturing, clustered nearby.

At the same time, according to Jacobs, Birmingham was "precisely the kind of city that seemed to have been outmoded by Manchester .... Birmingham ... had no specialty of the kind that made Manchester's economy so comprehensible .... But as it turned out Manchester was not the city of the future and Birmingham was .... Manchester had acquired the efficiency of a company town. Birmingham had retained something different: a high rate of innovation. Indeed, Birmingham and London are the only two cities in Britain today that retain a significant capacity to create new work from their existing work .... "

Jacobs' discussion of Manchester and Birmingham strongly suggests that the goals of economic development must go beyond "increased jobs and income." More jobs, more income, regional exports and a substantial contribution to Britain's Gross National Product were not enough to sustain Manchester through time.

Despite several decades of preoccupation with economic development, there is still no commonly accepted definition of what it means to be "developed." Today, development is determined by comparing one community to another in terms of gross output.

A more useful approach is to identify the dynamic qualities that differentiate communities that are self-renewing through time despite technological and economic change from communities that are not. What differentiates a Manchester from a Birmingham? What kinds of qualities in a community lead to the continuing formation of the material opportunities needed as markets and technologies change? These are important questions as we attempt to rekindle the self-renewing qualities of the U.S. economy and its older industrial "Manchesters."

ASSESSING DEVELOPMENT POLICY

The qualities that have distinguished Birmingham from Manchester, and which have characterized communities with long records of adapting to events, are *resilience, creativity, initiative-taking* and, above all, *diversity*. The ability to absorb abrupt changes in the economic, social and political environment and to bounce back; the ability to generate anew and to experiment; the desire and ability to begin and carry through useful projects; and a variety of enterprises that assure that no single event can affect the whole community—all simultaneously describe the self-renewing community. And all are characteristic of or generated by entrepreneurship.

Entrepreneurship, as measured by company formations, is a positive response to the environment, an expression of resilience. Every company formation is a creative act and bears with it an innovation in terms of product, service, way of doing business, location or appearance. Every company formation is the result of initiative-taking. Every new company adds to the diversity of a community, and the more widespread the kinds of company formations, the greater the diversity. A good case can be made that the number of company formations, the rate of their formation, the survival rate of new companies and their diversity provide good measures of a community's capacity to renew itself.

Economic development policies and programs that measure their objectives solely in terms of jobs and income do little to achieve these qualities, often prevent their development, and tend to make a community hostage to the decisions of only a few firms. Typically, a city or regional development authority launches an intensive campaign to attract large industrial plants to generate jobs and income. Many concessions are offered to the companies being wooed, including tax breaks, free or cheap land, long-term and low-interest loans, buildings, utility development, highway construction and railroad spurs.

Yet the probability of attracting a plant is not realistically considered and the consequences of attracting a major plant are not completely understood. One study conducted in the late 1950s—long before industry attraction efforts became as widespread as they are today—found some 16,000 development organizations competing for 200 available corporate moves at a cost of well over $250 million.

If the effort to obtain a plant succeeds, the incoming company will probably bring its own managers and highly skilled workers, while the community provides the low-cost, unskilled workers. A flow is set up in which the community's skilled, professionally trained youth leave for other cities while its unskilled youth are retained. An in-migrating company, attracted by cheap labor and low costs, can thus lower the net quality of a community's human resources.

With a large in-migrant company comes an enlarged work force and increased demand for municipal services such as police and fire protection, education and waste disposal. Since the incoming company has typically been given financial concessions, however, it is freed from paying its fair share of the tax revenues needed to provide these additional services.

Finally, the incoming company makes the community vulnerable. The community adjusts to the dominant source of jobs and income in the community and becomes hostage to it. This vulnerability becomes apparent when a distant, "objective" management decides to shift its production to a region with lower labor costs. In Ireland, for example, development officials have recruited some 250 foreign-owned plants that account for over 50 percent of the country's Gross National Product. Economic decisions affecting half the Irish economy are now being made in London, Frankfurt, New York and Tokyo.

Considering the economic and social consequences of dependence on a single crop, industry or resource (be it a mineral deposit or cheap manpower), the extent of local development efforts to attract a single corporate division to employ "cheap" labor is surprising. A recent example of the long-term negative effects of importing industrial plants to a region can be found in the Mexican-American border program. In ten years, the program attracted some 450 American manufacturers with the bait of low-cost labor. Now that wages are improving—they are still low by any standard—the companies are leaving for Central America, the Far East and Ireland where wages are even lower. The years 1974–1975 witnessed a 30 percent decrease in employment in the area, as 25 to 40 percent of the in-migrant American plants closed down, moved to other regions or severely reduced their operations, leaving serious social and political problems in their wake.

Instead of trying to attract branch operations of older, established firms, economic development policies should be more concerned with new and developing firms. They should aim at diversity and reduced dependence in any community or region on one or a few sectors of economic activity. Rather than concentrating on specific firms, they should focus on creating the ecological conditions conducive to new company formations.

Economic development policies emphasizing new firm formations rather than relocations provide a relatively lower risk, lower cost, actuarial approach that is less subject to failure because it is not project oriented. It is concerned with establishing conditions propitious to company formations rather than with financing and servicing specific plants or industries.

NEW POLICY CRITERIA

Programs for developing entrepreneurship must be based on what is known about entrepreneurs and company formation. Entrepreneurial behavior is denoted by a strong desire for independence, a predisposition to act, initiative-taking and risk-taking. Consequently, programs that are designed to prescribe in detail, control tightly and provide "what the entrepreneur truly needs" are contra-entrepreneurial by their very nature.

New companies are formed in an existing social, political and economic environment and so must adapt to that environment. The fewer changes that new companies require in their environments, the easier it is for them to survive. Consequently, policies designed to take full advantage of established institutions, rather than create new ones, have the greatest likelihood of success.

Revised policies should be premised on the "principle of the least": programs should lay claim to the least resources, regulations and procedures to achieve their goals. Entrepreneurially oriented policies and programs should be based on a "first-come, first-served" rather than "worst-first" basis. And they should take advantage of existing forces to elicit entrepreneurship rather than attempt to drive the process.

Communities and corporate management have become hostage to large organizations because of the number of workers concerned, the enormous investments already made and the local impacts of payrolls. New policies and programs are urgently needed to extend economies of small scale and significantly increase the efficiency of smaller units. . . .

For concerned public officials, a program for encouraging entre-preneurial formations is a low-risk, high potential-gain strategy. It removes direct public sector concern about the failure or success of specific enterprises, and shifts attention and responsibility to the aggregate of failures and successes. Unlike programs to attract large, expensive, long-term, highly visible projects that often depend upon major public works expenditures, policies and programs designed to encourage entrepreneurial events would distribute economic and political risks over a larger and less visible number of small firms. The larger the number of company formations, the higher the probability of some successes and the lower the potential loss of both resources and political coinage.

SINGLE-TECHNOLOGY STRATEGY

Most current public interest in entrepreneurship is focused on so-called high-technology companies. It is a mistake to take so narrow a view. Indeed, from a social viewpoint, the new company itself is the effective innovation, the matrix for new products and new jobs.

To concentrate on what a company is organized to produce and/or sell makes the implicit assumption that "things" have lives of their own. In effect, a high-technology orientation places the focus of policy on identifying the "right" technologies rather than on identifying the people and situations that lend themselves to success-ful entrepreneurship. What if the technology supported is suddenly displaced by another technology? What if the technology is too early by five years? If a company is supported on the basis of its technol-ogy, we are reluctant to see the company produce and sell something else. Instead, we throw more resources into a bad situation or withdraw support from an entrepreneurial entity that could well do something else that is valuable and profitable.

Yet many companies that start out to exploit some new technology eventually achieve success in a completely different field. One company starting out in aerospace technology switched to manufacturing a successful ski binding invented by its founder. Was the company a failure from a public policy viewpoint? Was the community enhanced or diminished?

Programs for promoting entrepreneurship in a community should not be targeted to a single technology. The policy focus should be on eliciting and attracting entrepreneurship in as wide a range of industrial sectors and businesses as possible in order to enhance diversity in the community.

DISPLACEMENT AS OPPORTUNITY

Major sectors in the American economy are in trouble, and thousands of workers are being laid off or losing their jobs permanently. As a result, communities and regions where troubled industries are concentrated are also becoming victims of economic and technological change. Public policy attempts to mitigate some of these changes. Yet these displacements can present opportunities to create new firms and build more diversified local economies that are less dependent upon one or a few large industries.

Studies of entrepreneurship provide convincing evidence that displacement is a key influence in the creation of new firms. . . .

Job dissatisfaction of various kinds is often cited by individuals who start new companies. . . .

Some "displacements" are generated primarily by the passage of time. One recurring stimulus for company formations is the "traumatic birthday." . . .

Another such displacement is rooted in the "empty-nest" syndrome experienced by the wife/mother whose children have left home. . . .

The challenge to public policy is to create the conditions that permit creative and resilient responses rather than passive, ameliorative programs that subsidize inaction by those displaced or by their communities. It would be both unacceptable and unethical to encourage dislocations in the interests of increasing the number of company formations in a region or locality. The years ahead, however, are likely to yield large numbers of displacements, and new policies and programs can be fielded to respond to them.

A national policy responding to major economic dislocations should include a central element encouraging company formations. Workers displaced by mass layoffs in the steel and auto industries, divorced and widowed women, retired people across the country—all are examples of persons being displaced in today's economy. Although only a few can become entrepreneurs, their numbers could be significantly enhanced by programs that educate people about the feasibility and desirability of forming a company and by programs that galvanize the resources and information required to support such actions.

Displacement can often be anticipated, as in the case of obsolescing plants and industries. National, regional, corporate and union programs aimed at eliciting company formations among those affected can be started long in advance of the event. Such programs would make the event less calamitous and increase the probability of company formations by preparing for them when stress is less immediate. That such a policy can be effective is demonstrated by the substantial number of companies formed by retirees without any preparation and by the historical evidence of the surge of company formations in the aftermath of disaster.

DESIGNING DEVELOPMENT POLICIES

Any policy that "tunes" the existing system to be more favorable to new and small businesses has far more potential for success than does one that depends on government-administered programs. One study revealed that a 1 percent shift in the loan portfolio of commercial banks in three states to the financing of new and small companies could have provided more than twice the effective capital per year than the combined amounts of all federal, state and local programs in effect at the time. Add to this the inherent delays and misjudgments in direct programs administered by non-entrepreneurs on behalf of entrepreneurs, and it is easy to see that the programs have little potential to achieve our purpose.

Instead, we need to reduce the obstacles to new company formation in terms of access to capital, regulatory complexity, management inadequacies, and general attitudes toward entrepreneurship in government, business, labor, the education establishment and the nation at large. Indeed, the time has come for the country as a whole to become entrepreneurially minded again: quick to spot opportunities, creative in taking advantage of them and sagacious in capitalizing on them.

FINANCING NEW COMPANIES

Perhaps the most severe problem faced by the nascent entrepreneur, the new company and the young company is obtaining adequate capital—capital required to bring the business into being, working capital needed to establish a foothold and capital required for growth.

More than 99 percent of all new businesses obtain their start-up funds from personal savings and relatives. The 500 to 600 venture capital firms in the United States each make about three investments per year, of which less than 15 percent have been in start-ups. The flurry of investment in high-technology start-ups during the past year ignores the capital needs of the estimated 600,000 to 1,000,000 other start-ups in the United States each year.

Policies for financial support of desirable company start-ups have been under intensive discussion during recent years. Many programs have been put in place, and their record of performance is mixed. Programs for direct funding of new and small businesses through new institutions such as development banks have been relatively unsuccessful wherever they have been tried. Any new institution has start-up problems, of course. Even more significant, however, government banking or funding institutions inexorably become quite cautious and conservative because they are dealing with publicly supplied and scrutinized funds and, in the end, they do not serve their purpose well.

The availability of financial support directly influences the level of entrepreneurial activity in a community: companies are formed when financial resources are readily available. Thus, in the early stages of company growth, the attitudes of local lending institutions play a critical role.

Empirical studies of how loan officers and private investors respond to new and small businesses have uncovered wide variations in the attitudes of loan officers within a given bank, of bankers and private investors within a given city, and of bankers and private investors in different communities. These findings suggest a strong need for policy options aimed at educating the financial community, making it aware of practices followed in other communities and developing information flows to ensure that no new or small company is turned away for the wrong reasons. This could be accomplished through special educational programs or an expert retrieval system. Under the retrieval system, a lender dealing with a new company whose product is unfamiliar to him would be connected, by phone, to another lender with expertise in that field.

Other policy options affecting the financial ecology of new and small companies are those designed to increase their flow of capital. Several proposals to increase the amount of both equity and working capital for new and small companies, without appropriating public funds, should be considered:

- changes in current law and regulations to enable increased investment by insurance companies and pension funds in new and small businesses;
- use of government deposits as an incentive for financial support of new and small businesses;
- encouragement of pooled loan programs to minimize risk while investing in new and small businesses, particularly in their need for services and infrastructure; and
- development of a two-tier, two-window interest rate system that provides loans to small companies at lower rates.

CONCLUSION

The time is ripe to discard bureaucratic approaches to economic development and focus instead on the creative and resilient attitudes that foster entrepreneurship. A society or community with a high level of entrepreneurship ultimately incurs less risk than one that relies upon the illusory security of large-scale enterprise. For only a large number of company formations, occurring continually over time, can help ensure the creativity and resilience that a community needs to respond to change and capitalize quickly on new opportunities.

Nature, through the evolutionary process, has established the durability and stability of diversity. We can learn from her.

C

UDAG CRITERIA
FOR SELECTION

The following criteria have been developed by the central office staff for the review, rating and ultimate selection of UDAG applications for approval:

1. Relative distress of the applicant.
2. Private leverage. The ratio of private investment to UDAG funds. The national average is now 6.2 to 1 and the ratio should be at least 5 to 1 to assure competitiveness. A ratio below 5 to 1 must be strongly supported by other factors and less than 2½ to 1 will not be considered.
3. Repayment of action grant to recipient. At least a portion of the grant should be returned to the city for recycling. The repayment may be structured as a "soft" second mortgage or lease so the developer virtually has a grant if the project is not successful.
4. Permanent jobs. Weight is given to the total number of new jobs created, the number of low/moderate income jobs created, and the ratio of UDAG funds to jobs created. Currently a cost of $5,000 or less per job created is considered competitive. Retained jobs are also important.
5. New taxes. New taxes created and the ratio of new taxes to Action Grant dollars. A return of $.10 per dollar is competitive.
6. Commitment to minority participation. The creation of minority jobs and the inclusion of minority entrepreneurs is weighted heavily.
7. Commitment to hire and train hard-core unemployed, especially through the use of CETA, is a plus factor.
8. Other public participation. Investment of funds by the state and/or city is a good measure of their support of the project.
9. Feasibility. The project must be feasible socially and economically and the participants should be capable of starting within one year of preliminary approval and completing the project within four years of that date.

The program seeks to fund an equal number of commercial, industrial, and neighborhood projects. To date, approvals have been 35% industrial, 34% commercial, and 30% neighborhood. Applicants compete with each other only within these categories, thus residential projects, which create comparatively few jobs, are not penalized.

Commitment letters should include the following information:
1. Commitment for a specified amount.
2. Commitment to a specific project.
3. Scheduled completion time.
4. Number of jobs created and/or retained.
5. Source of funds.
6. Terms of the loan, if any.
7. If a private lender is involved, letter must state that lender has reviewed the project and found it to be economically feasible.
8. The "but for" statement. "Our commitment to make the aforementioned investment is contingent upon the receipt of the action grant, and, but for the receipt of the action grant requested, we would not make the previously stated commitment."
9. An expression of willingness to sign a legally binding contract upon award of the grant.

Bank pool letters must state that the credit of the individual borrowers "has been approved and the following commitments are hereby made available." A recitation of the terms of each loan should follow.

Letters from mortgage brokers are not acceptable unless they contain a definite commitment from the lender setting forth all of the terms of the loan. A letter direct from the lender is preferable. Letters from mortgage brokers will not be accepted as a legally binding commitment.

Investment brokers letters must state unequivocally that the firm will underwrite or purchase the entire issue to be acceptable. "Best efforts" letters will not do.

D
FINANCIAL RATIOS

Profitability ratios		Norm
Gross margin	$$\frac{\text{Sales} - \text{Cost of goods sold}}{\text{Sales}}$$	20%
Profit margins	$$\frac{\text{Earnings before interest and taxes}}{\text{Sales}}$$	8%
	$$\frac{\text{Net profit}}{\text{Sales}}$$	5%
Return on total investment	$$\frac{\text{Earnings before interest and taxes}}{\text{Total assets}}$$	15%
	$$\frac{\text{Net profit}}{\text{Total assets}}$$	10%
Capitalization rate	$$\frac{\text{Net cash flow} + \text{Debt service}}{\text{Invested equity} + \text{Debt}}$$	15%
Return on equity	$$\frac{\text{Net profit}}{\text{Net worth}}$$	20%
Cash-on-cash rate of return	$$\frac{\text{Net cash flow}}{\text{Invested equity}}$$	20%
Activity ratios		
Total asset turnover	$$\frac{\text{Sales}}{\text{Total assets}}$$	2X
Fixed asset turnover	$$\frac{\text{Sales}}{\text{Fixed assets}}$$	3X

Liquidity ratios		Norm
Current ratio	$\dfrac{\text{Current assets}}{\text{Current liabilities}}$	2:1
Quick ratio	$\dfrac{\text{Cash + Marketable securities + Acc'ts. rec.}}{\text{Current liabilities}}$	1:1

Note: Working capital = current assets − current liabilities

Solvency ratios		
Debt-equity ratio	$\dfrac{\text{Total liabilities}}{\text{Net worth}}$	1:1
	$\dfrac{\text{Long-term liabilities}}{\text{Net worth}}$	0.7:1
Debt ratio	$\dfrac{\text{Total liabilities}}{\text{Total assets}}$	0.5:1
Debt coverage ratio	$\dfrac{\text{Earnings before taxes}}{\text{Interest + Fixed obligations}}$	4X
	$\dfrac{\text{Net profit}}{\text{Long-term debt}}$	20%
	$\dfrac{\text{Net operating income}}{\text{Debt service}}$	1.3:1
Loan coverage ratio	$\dfrac{\text{Loan}}{\text{Asset value*}}$	0.7:1

---

*Some lenders use project cost instead of value.

E
OVERVIEW OF MARKET STUDIES

**MARKET STUDY OUTLINE FOR A
SPECULATIVE OFFICE COMPLEX**

Introduction

    Overview of the market study

    Review of data sources

    Disclaimer

Summary of findings and recommendations

Community description

    Location

    Transportation

    Education

    Medical services

    Recreation and cultural activities

    Communications

    Government

Market area identification

    Primary area

    Secondary area

    Economic analysis

        Labor force and employment

        Place of work

        Occupational structure

        Unemployment

        Population tends and characteristics

Demand projections

    Employment projections

    Office space demand projections

[Demand projections]

> Office space supply
>
> > Existing
> >
> > Planned additions
>
> Excess demand projections
>
> Capture rates by major market sub-area
>
> > Project capture rate
> >
> > Sensitivity analysis of different project capture rates
>
> Historic absorption of office space by sub-area

Site analysis

> Location
>
> Area development
>
> Zoning and physical characteristics

Comparables

> For each complex: location, age, size, overall average rents, absorption, vacancy, unit size range, and tenant mix
>
> Inventory of office development by year and sub-area

MARKET STUDY OUTLINE
FOR A NEW LOCAL BANK

Statement of objectives

> Why the study is being undertaken and for whom
>
> Qualifications of the analysts

The geographic area

> Brief description of the region and urban areas relevant to the banking business

Market area identification

> The primary service area (PSA)—the area that will generate 75 percent of all loans and deposits
>
> Delineation of the PSA
>
> > Driving times
> >
> > Traffic flow patterns

[Market area identification; delineation of the PSA]

    Traffic barriers

    Future transportation plans

  PSA characteristics

    Residential development patterns and prospects

    Commercial development patterns and prospects

    Industrial development patterns and prospects

  Competing banks and bank branches in the PSA

Demand estimation

  Population, current and projected

  Income, current and projected

  Retail sales, current and projected

  Recent construction activity

  Area employment, current

    Major employers

    Employment by occupation

    Place of employment

Analysis of comparables

  Estimating the success of new local banks
    in other parts of the state

  Existing banks in the PSA

    Current deposits

    Distance from proposed bank site

    History of existing banking office location

Estimating total deposits for the PSA

  Regression models estimating deposits as a function of
    population, income, retail sales, and other factors

  Selection of reasonable, conservative estimates of deposits

Estimating market share of deposits for the proposed bank

  Share of market per bank

  Share of market per location

[Estimating market share of deposits]

 Conservative estimate of market share

 Estimated distribution of deposits by type of account

Summary of major points

Map of the PSA

Photographs of all branches in the PSA

BIBLIOGRAPHY

BASIC REFERENCES for Chapter 1

Arndt, H. W. 1981. "Economic Development: A Semantic History." *Economic Development and Cultural Change* 29 (April):457-66.

Friedmann, John, and Alonso, W., eds. 1964. *Regional Development and Planning: A Reader.* Cambridge, MA: MIT Press.

Friedmann, John, and Alonso, W., eds. 1975. *Regional Policy: Readings in Theory and Applications.* Cambridge, MA: MIT Press.

Hansen, Niles M., ed. 1972. *Growth Centers in Regional Economic Development.* New York: Free Press.

Isard, Walter. 1975. *Introduction to Regional Science.* Englewood Cliffs, NJ: Prentice-Hall.

Knight, Frank H. 1971. *Risk, Uncertainty and Profit.* Chicago: University of Chicago Press (originally published 1921).

Miernyk, William. 1982. *Regional Analysis and Regional Policy.* Cambridge, MA: Oelgeschlager, Gunn and Hain.

Perloff, Harvey S., et al. 1960. *Regions, Resources and Economic Growth.* Lincoln: University of Nebraska Press.

Thompson, Wilbur R. 1965. *A Preface to Urban Economics.* Baltimore, MD: Johns Hopkins Press.

Vaughan, Roger J. 1977. *The Urban Impacts of Federal Policies: Volume 2, Economic Development.* Santa Monica, CA: Rand.

Vietorisz, Thomas, and Harrison, Bennett. 1970. *The Economic Development of Harlem.* New York: Praeger.

DEVELOPMENT PLANNING: References for Chapter 2

Bendavid-Val, Avrom. 1980. *Local Economic Development: From Goals to Projects.* Planning Advisory Service Report number 353. Chicago: American Planning Association.

Bryson, J. M., and Delbecq, A. L. 1979. "A Contingent Approach to Strategy and Tactics in Project Planning." *Journal of the American Planning Association* 45 (April):167–79.

Drucker, Peter F. 1974. *Management: Tasks, Responsibilities and Practice*. New York: Harper and Row.

Friedman, Stephen B. 1979. "Economic Development: The Planning Response." In *The Practice of Local Government Planning*. Frank S. So, Israel Stollman, Frank Beal, and David S. Arnold (eds.). Washington, DC: International City Management Association, pp. 589–99.

Galloway, T. D. 1979. "Comment." *Journal of the American Planning Association* 45 (October 1979):399–403.

Kaufman, J. L. 1979. "Comment." *Journal of the American Planning Association* 45 (October):403–406.

Levin, Richard I. 1981. *The Executive's Illustrated Primer of Long-Range Planning*. Englewood Cliffs, NJ: Prentice-Hall.

Linneman, Robert E. 1980. *Shirt-Sleeve Approach to Long-Range Planning for the Smaller Growing Corporation*. Englewood Cliffs, NJ: Prentice-Hall.

Linneman, Robert E., and Chandran, R. 1981. "Contingency Planning: A Key to Swift Managerial Action in the Uncertain Tomorrow." *Managerial Planning* 29 (January/February):23–27.

Malizia, Emil. 1982. "Contingency Planning for Local Economic Development." *Environment and Planning B* 9 (June):163–76.

O'Connor, Rochelle. 1978. *Planning Under Uncertainty: Multiple Scenarios and Contingency Planning*. New York: Conference Board.

Steiner, George A. 1979. *Strategic Planning: What Every Manager Must Know*. New York: Free Press.

DEVELOPMENT TECHNIQUES: References for Chapter 2

Bendavid-Val, Avrom. 1983. *Regional and Local Economic Analysis for Practitioners*. New York: Praeger.

Czamanski, Stan. 1972. *Regional Science Techniques in Practice*. Lexington, MA: D. C. Heath.

Hirschhorn, Larry. 1980. "Scenario Writing: A Developmental Approach." *Journal of the American Planning Association* 46 (April):172–83.

Isard, Walter. 1960. *Methods of Regional Analysis*. Cambridge, MA: MIT Press.

Linstone, H. A., and Simmons, W. H. 1977. *Futures Research: New Directions*. Reading, MA: Addison-Wesley.

Richardson, Harry W. 1972. *Input-Output and Regional Economics*. New York: Wiley.

Shah, Praful B. "Economic Base Studies: Elements, Forecasting, Fiscal Impact, Evaluation." In *The Practice of Local Government Planning*. Frank S. So, Israel Stollman, Frank Beal, and David S. Arnold (eds.). Washington, DC: International City Management Association, pp. 599–613.

Stevens, Benjamin H., and Moore, Craig L. 1980. "A Critical Review of the Literature on Shift-Share as a Forecasting Technique." *Journal of Regional Science* 20 (December):419–37.

ECONOMIC DEVELOPMENT THEORIES:
References for Chapter 3

Friedmann, John, and Weaver, Clyde. 1979. *Territory and Function: The Evolution of Regional Planning*. Berkeley: University of California Press. Theoretical overview, growth theory, growth poles, dependency theory.

Hirschman, Albert O. 1958. *The Strategy of Economic Development*. New Haven: Yale University Press. Classic discussion of economic development and unbalanced growth—polarization and trickle-down effects.

Hoover, Edgar M. 1971. *An Introduction to Regional Economics*. New York: Knopf. Economic base theory, backward and forward linkage.

Jacobs, Jane. 1969. *The Economy of Cities*. New York: Random House. Role of innovation and entrepreneurship in economic development.

Malizia, Emil, and Reid, Dianne. 1976. "Perspectives and Strategies for U.S. Regional Development." *Growth and Change* 7 (October):41–47. Theory-based development strategies.

Myrdal, Gunnar. 1957. *Economic Theory and Underdeveloped Regions*. New York: Harper Torchbooks. Spread and backwash effects; unbalanced growth.

Norton, R. D., and Rees, J. 1979. "The Product Cycle and the Spatial Decentralization of American Manufacturing." *Regional Studies* 13:141-51. Application of product cycle theory.

Ohlin, Bertil. 1967. *Interregional and International Trade*. Rev. ed. Cambridge, MA: Harvard University Press. Seminal work on interregional trade.

Parr, John B. 1973. "Growth Poles, Regional Development, and Central Place Theory." *Papers, Regional Science Association* 31:173-212. Overview of growth poles in spatial development.

Pred, Allan. 1976. "The Interurban Transmission of Growth in Advanced Economies: Empirical Findings Versus Regional-Planning Assumptions." *Regional Studies* 10:151-71. Challenge to growth pole and growth center views of the diffusion process.

Rhodes, Robert I., ed. 1970. *Imperialism and Underdevelopment: A Reader*. New York: Monthly Review Press. Good collection of articles on imperialism and dependency theories.

Richardson, Harry W. 1973. *Regional Growth Theory*. London: Macmillan Press. Overview of regional growth and development theories.

Schumpeter, Joseph A. 1962. *Capitalism, Socialism and Democracy*. New York: Harper Torchbooks. One of Schumpeter's discussions of the role of the entrepreneur in capitalist development.

Shapero, Albert. 1981. "Entrepreneurship: Key to Self-Renewing Economies." *Commentary* 5 (April):19-23. New company formation and resilient local economies.

Thompson, Wilbur. 1968. "Internal and External Factors in the Development of Urban Economics." In *Issues in Urban Economics*. Harvey S. Perloff and Lowden Wingo, Jr. (eds.). Baltimore, MD: Johns Hopkins Press, pp. 43-62. Initiation and diffusion of economic growth in a system of cities.

Uathavikul, P. 1966. "Decision Theory and Regional Economic Growth." Ph.D. dissertation, Cornell University. Explanation of economic base theory, sector theory, and stages theory.

Vernon, Raymond. 1966. "International Investment and International Trade in the Product Cycle." *Quarterly Review of Economics* 80 (May):190-207. Product cycle theory.

DEVELOPMENT STRATEGIES: References for Chapter 3

Armington, Catherine, and Odle, Marjorie. 1982. "Sources of Job Growth: A New Look at the Small Business Role." *Commentary* 6 (Fall):3-7.

Bangs, Andy, and Osgood, William R. 1978. *Business Planning Guide*. Portsmouth, NH: Upstart Publishing Company.

Bergman, Edward M. 1981. "Local Economic Development Planning in an Era of Capital Mobility." *Carolina Planning* 7 (Fall):29-37.

Conroy, Michael E. 1975. *Regional Economic Growth: Diversification and Control*. New York: Praeger.

Malizia, Emil, and Rubin, Sarah. 1983. "Taking Care of Business: Emerging Economic Development Practice in Smaller Cities." Unpublished monograph.

Malizia, Emil, and Rubin, Sarah. 1982. "New Strategies for Rural Economic Development." *Carolina Planning* 8 (Summer):39-46.

Redburn, F. Stevens, and Buss, Terry F., eds. 1982. *Public Policies for Distressed Communities*. Lexington, MA: D. C. Heath. Part IV: "Plant Closings and Responses."

Regional Planning Commission. 1981. *Catalog of Concepts on Management and Technical Assistance Services*. Louisiana Conference on Small Business Innovation. New Orleans.

U.S. Conference of Mayors. 1980. *Local Economic Development Tools and Techniques*. Washington: U.S. Department of Housing and Urban Development and U.S. Department of Commerce.

DEVELOPMENT FINANCING: References for Chapter 4

Barker, Michael, ed. 1983. *Financing State and Local Economic Development*. Durham, NC: Duke University Press.

Bearse, Peter J., ed. 1978. "Mobilizing Capital for Economic Development: Institutional Innovation and the New Urban Policy." The Center for New Jersey Affairs, Woodrow Wilson School of Public and International Affairs. August.

Bourgeois, Thomas G. 1982. "Development Finance Concepts and State Development Activities." Unpublished departmental paper. Chapel Hill, NC:

Department of City and Regional Planning, University of North Carolina at Chapel Hill.

Corporation for Enterprise Development. 1984. "Investing in Entrepreneurship." *The Entrepreneurial Economy* 2 (January):13-17.

CUED. *Guide to Federal Economic Development Programs*. Washington, DC: National Council for Urban Economic Development.

Council of State Planning Agencies. 1981. "Financing Entrepreneurship: A Review of the Issues and Recent State Innovations." March.

Friedman, Robert, and Schweke, William, eds. 1981. *Expanding the Opportunity to Produce: Revitalizing the American Economy Through New Enterprise Development*. Washington, DC: Corporation for Enterprise Development.

Hansen, Derek. 1980. *Banking and the Finance of Small Business*. Washington, DC: Council of State Planning Agencies.

Litvak, Lawrence. 1981. *Pension Funds and Economic Renewal*. Washington, DC: Council of State Planning Agencies.

Litvak, Lawrence, and Daniels, Beldon. 1979. *Innovations in Development Finance*. Washington, DC: Council of State Planning Agencies.

Pfeffer, Irving, ed. 1967. *The Financing of Small Business: A Current Assessment.* New York: Macmillan.

Region Planning Commission. 1981. *Catalog of Concepts on Capital Formation and Development Finance*. Louisiana Conference on Small Business Innovation. New Orleans.

Richards, Judith W. 1983. *Fundamentals of Development Finance: A Practitioner's Guide*. New York: Praeger.

Vogt, John A. 1983. *A Guide to Municipal Leasing*. Chicago: Municipal Finance Officers Association.

PROJECT PLANNING: References for Chapter 5

Bangs, Andy, and Osgood, William R. 1978. *Business Planning Guide*. Portsmouth, NH: Upstart Publishing.

Baum, Warren C. 1970. "The Project Cycle." *Finance & Development* 7 (June). Reprint.

Baum, Warren C. 1978. "The World Bank Project Cycle." *Finance & Development* 15 (December):10–17.

Mahmood, S. T., and Ghosh, A. K., eds. 1979. "Handbook for Community Economic Development." East Los Angeles, CA: Community Research Group, The East Los Angeles Community Union (TELACU). See especially Chapter 3.

Rondinelli, Dennis A., ed. 1977. *Planning Development Projects*. Stroudsburg, PA: Dowden, Hutchinson & Ross.

Rubel, Stanley M., ed. 1977. *Guide to Venture Capital Sources*, 4th ed. Wellesley Hills, MA: Capital Publishing.

Sugden, Robert, and Williams, Alan. 1978. *The Principles of Practical Cost-Benefit Analysis*. Oxford: Oxford University Press.

Vogt, A. John. 1977. *Capital Improvement Programming: A Handbook for Local Government Officials*. Chapel Hill, NC: Institute of Government.

BUSINESS DEVELOPMENT FINANCING:
References for Chapter 6

Barry, Peter J., Hopkin, John A., and Baker, C. B. 1979. *Financial Management in Agriculture*, 2nd ed. Danville, IL: Interstate Printers & Publishers.

Dixon, Robert L. 1982. *The Executive's Accounting Primer*, 2d ed. New York: McGraw-Hill.

Martin, Thomas J. 1980. *Financing the Growing Business*. New York: Holt, Rinehart and Winston.

Martin, Thomas J., and Gustafson, Mark. 1980. *Valuing Your Business*. New York: Holt, Rinehart and Winston.

"A Note on Financial Analysis." Harvard Business School 9-206-047, Revised 1/80. Distributed by HBS Case Services, Boston, MA.

Pritchard, Robert E. 1977. *Operational Financial Management*. Englewood Cliffs, NJ: Prentice-Hall.

Welsch, Glenn A., and Anthony, Robert N. 1981. *Fundamentals of Financial Accounting*, 3rd ed. Homewood, IL: Richard D. Irwin.

Zwick, Jack. 1975. *A Handbook of Small Business Finance*. Small Business Management series no. 15. Washington, DC: Small Business Administration.

REAL ESTATE DEVELOPMENT FINANCING:
References for Chapter 6

Britton, James A., Jr., and Kerwood, Lewis O. 1977. *Financing Income-Producing Real Estate: A Theory and Casebook*. New York: McGraw-Hill.

Brueggeman, William B., and Stone, Leo D. 1981. *Real Estate Finance*, 7th ed. Homewood, IL: Richard D. Irwin.

Howardsoft, Inc. 1982. *Real Estate Analyzer*, 2nd ed. La Jolla, CA: Howard Software Services.

Howell, Joseph T. 1984. *Real Estate Development Syndication.* New York: Praeger.

International Association of Assessing Officers. 1978. *Improving Real Estate Assessment: A Reference Manual*. Washington, DC: IAAO.

Pyhrr, Stephen A., and Cooper, James R. 1982. *Real Estate Investment: Strategy, Analysis, Decisions*. Boston: Warren, Gorham & Lamont.

MARKET AND FEASIBILITY ANALYSIS:
References for Chapter 8

General

Applebaum, William. 1966. "Methods for Determining Store Trade Areas: Market Penetration and Potential Sales." *Journal of Marketing Research* 3 (May):127–41.

Applebaum, William. 1970. *Shopping Center Strategy: A Case Study of Planning, Location and Development of the Del Monte Center, Monterey, California*. New York: International Council of Shopping Centers.

Churchill, Gilbert A., Jr. 1983. *Marketing Research: Methodological Foundations*, 3rd ed. Chicago: Dryden Press.

Downs, Anthony. 1966. "Characteristics of Various Economic Studies." *The Appraisal Journal* 34 (July):329–38.

Huff, David L. 1964. "Defining and Estimating a Trading Area." *Journal of Marketing* 28 (July):34–38.

McCarthy, E. Jerome. 1981. *Basic Marketing: A Managerial Approach*, 7th ed. Homewood, IL: Richard D. Irwin.

Nelson, Richard L. 1958. *The Selection of Retail Locations*. New York: F. W. Dodge Corporation.

Reilly, William J. 1931. *The Law of Retail Gravitation*. New York: Knickerbocker Press.

Ruddick, Morris E., Sherwood, Philip K., and Stevens, Robert E. 1983. *The Marketing Research Handbook: A Decision-Oriented Approach*. Englewood Cliffs, NJ: Prentice-Hall.

Young, G. I. M. 1970. "Feasibility Studies." *The Appraisal Journal* 38 (July): 376–83.

Real Estate Development

Barrett, G. Vincent, and Blair, John P. 1982. *How to Conduct and Analyze Real Estate Market and Feasibility Studies*. New York: Van Nostrand and Reinhold.

Cooper, James R., and Gunterman, Karl L. 1974. *Real Estate and Urban Land Analysis*. Lexington, MA: D. C. Heath.

Graaskamp, James A. 1980. *A Guide to Feasibility Analysis*. Chicago: Society of Real Estate Appraisers.

Graaskamp, James A. 1981. *Fundamentals of Real Estate Development*. Washington, DC: Urban Land Institute.

Messner, Steven E., et al. 1977. *Analyzing Real Estate Opportunities: Market and Feasibility Studies*. Chicago: National Association of Realtors.

Roddenwig, Richard J., and Shlaes, Jared. 1984. *Analyzing the Economic Feasibility of a Development Project*. Planning Advisory Service Report no. 380. Chicago: American Planning Association.

Stout, Gary E., and Vitl, Joseph E. 1982. "Public Incentives and Financing Techniques for Codevelopment." Washington, DC: Urban Land Institute.

Business Development

Barnes, James G., and Noonam, A. C. 1982. "Marketing Research: Some Basics for Small Business." *Journal of Small Business Management* 20 (July):62–66.

"Business Growth." 1983. *The Business Owner* 7 (November):4–7.

Lee, Donald D. 1978. *Industrial Marketing Research: Techniques and Practices*. Westport: Technomic Publishing.

Mancuso, Joseph R. 1983. *How to Prepare and Present a Business Plan*. New York: Prentice-Hall.

Measuring Markets: A Guide to the Use of Federal and State Statistical Data. 1979. Washington, DC: U.S. Department of Commerce, Industry and Trade Administration.

Patterson, Larry T., and McCullough. 1980. "A Market Study Methodology for Small Business." *Journal of Small Business Management* 18 (July):30–36.

Schweser, Carl. 1982. "A Quick Test of Financial Reality for Would-Be Entrepreneurs." *Journal of Small Business Management* 20 (October):78–81.

Stevens, Robert E., and Sherwood, Philip K. 1982. *How to Prepare a Feasibility Study*. Englewood Cliffs, NJ: Prentice-Hall.

REFERENCES FOR CHAPTER 9

Goodman, Robert. 1979. *The Last Entrepreneurs*. New York: Simon and Schuster.

Jacobs, Jane. 1984. *Cities and the Wealth of Nations*. New York: Random House.

Miller, James P. 1983. "Interstate Competition for Business: Changing Roles of Federal and State Initiatives." Economic Development Division, Economic Research Service, U.S. Department of Agriculture, December.

INDEX

ABOUT THE AUTHOR

EMIL E. MALIZIA is an associate professor of city and regional planning at the University of North Carolina at Chapel Hill. He has taught the theories, strategies, and techniques of economic development to graduate students and practicing professionals since 1969. He also has extensive policy research experience and numerous publications on urban, rural, and regional development. He has been a senior Fulbright scholar in Colombia, South America, and a special assistant in the Employment and Training Administration of the U.S. Department of Labor. Most recently, he has designed and initiated economic development projects as a consultant to businesses, developers, and governments in the southeast.

Dr. Malizia brings to this book over 20 years of domestic and international experience in the field of local economic development. He holds an M.R.P. and Ph.D. from Cornell University.

DATE DUE

DEMCO 38-297